Be Happy
Life After Loss

A Memoir

Susen I. Hickman

Azalea Art Press
Southern Pines, NC

ISBN: 978-0-9849760-7-2

Library of Congress Control Number:
2013950280

Cover art: acrylic on canvas
and poppy line drawing
by Susen I. Hickman

Dedication

My angels in Heaven
Dave and Michele
who lift me up

My angels on Earth
Mike and Matt
who keep me grounded

Contents

Introduction

It has never been my dream or ambition to be a serious or published author. Except for writing this memoir, it still is not. But after the passing of my husband, Dave, I sought books that would give me some comfort in the knowledge that I was not alone in losing a husband far too early in life, and that I was far from the first woman to manage a life after loss.

What I discovered were books that fell short of how other women felt about the simple things that confronted me. I was searching for the common emotions among those who have lost a loved one that tie us together in our everyday lives. My experience going to the grocery store is a prime example. Sounds so simple, doesn't it? But why didn't everyone in the store understand what I was going through? What did I want there and how was it I could leave without buying anything?

About the same time as the loss of my husband, a very well-known author had written a book about her loss. It was beautifully written and people raved about it, rightly so. It did tell a wonderful story. For me however, it fell short of telling me what I needed to know—that I was not alone in the feelings that washed over me, and that what I was feeling was normal. How did others handle the pain of loss and how did they find a way to continue on with a new life? These were just some of the questions that confronted me, and after years of journal writing and trying to find my own peace, I now share my story with you through this memoir.

I could not have written this memoir without also writing about the loss of my daughter, Michele. She passed at the age of seventeen from cancer after having been diagnosed and undergoing several surgeries and radiation starting at the tender age of thirteen.

I cannot tell you how many people have said to me—and maybe you've heard this yourself, "You should write a book." Sounds so simple, but it has been seven years since the day I first began journaling until the completion of this memoir. Many times I have set it aside, feeling its contents too personal to share. Why would I want to expose my feelings to everyone who picks up this book?

The answer is pretty simple. It is my hope that perhaps someone who reads this will feel a shared connection with me and others who have survived loss and know that they are not alone in the feelings that overwhelm them. This may also reach a person who is looking for some insight into what someone they know might be experiencing after loss.

As you read my story, it will not be

your story; your loves not my loves, but perhaps the connectedness that makes us all human can be shared. I hope you will relate in similar ways, however small, to the feelings I experienced of love, loss, emptiness, fortitude, gratitude and the attempts of living life with purpose and fulfillment. It's an age-old story told one more time. How did I survive life after loss? And then, what did I do?

- Susen I. Hickman
September, 2013

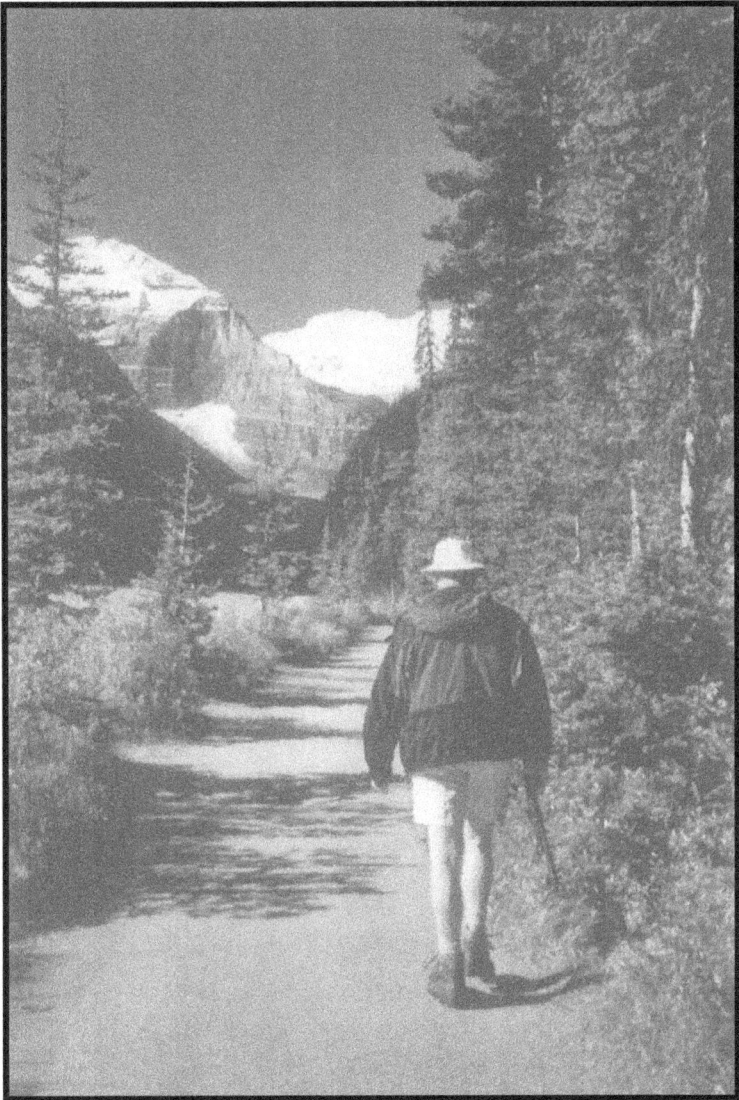

Gone Hiking
(July 27, 1946 - May 22, 2005)

Chapter I
The Day

Just one week before the day that would change my life forever, Dave had finished tiling the floor in our large family room. The ceiling is two stories high and, at one end of the room, there is a thick timbered ladder climbing to a loft where our children Michele, Mike and Matt played on a Commodore 64 in their youth.

Tiling the floor had been a huge project and took Dave literally forever to finish. He had attacked the project in his usual approach to getting things done: take your time and do it right—a little bit here, a little bit there and eventually the task would get finished. This floor was so large the whole project bordered on being ridiculous as month after month rolled by while he laid tile in different sections of the room. I knew it would get done, but when?

So now the floor was finally finished and that afternoon, as a finishing touch to the room, he applied the last coat of paint to the walls. "Can't have a new floor without repainting the walls!" he said. It was a job well done, and done on his terms. Who would have imagined on the very day this project was completed and as the sun folded into the Earth that his chair would sit there—empty?

Now I sit in the companion chair next to his and my mind reluctantly moves to the day seven years ago when I felt the sun would never rise again, the clock had stopped and time did not exist.

We had just returned from taking his mother to brunch at Saul's, one of our favorite little deli restaurants in Berkeley, California. The brunch was in memory of her sister who had died two months prior to this day on what would have been her ninety-third birthday. Afterward, Dave wandered into the family room. "I have to touch up the paint on this wall," he said. It was the last small detail that needed his attention before the room was finally finished. "Then I think I'll watch sports on TV and rest. I don't think brunch agreed with me. I'm feeling a little off."

"Fine," I said. "I'm going to run to the store and pick up some things for dinner. I'll only be a few minutes. Matt will be home soon. You promised him you'd help him replace the ceiling light fixture in his room," I reminded him. I leaned over him as he sat in his chair and gave him a quick kiss. As I walked out of the family room heading toward the front door he called to me, "Hey, I love you."

I returned from the store about forty-five minutes later. Our son, Matt, who was twenty-three at the time, met me at the front door. "Mom, is Dad okay? I just got home a second ago and he's sitting in his chair in the family room but he doesn't look well."

Not being particularly alarmed—whoever thinks the worst?—I unpacked two bags of groceries, putting eggs and meat in the refrigerator and stowing cans in the pantry. Then I headed to the family room, and as I walked in I glanced at Dave. It was one of those surreal moments in time when you know where you are, but you feel as if you are on the outside looking through a window into someone else's life.

I found Dave taking a Sunday afternoon nap, his arms resting comfortably on the arms of the chair, legs stretched out in front of him and crossed at the ankles. It was the same routine scene that had played out many times on any given weekend in front of our TV as he watched some sporting event. But this time he wasn't sleeping. I knew it as surely as I knew it was a Sunday in May. I'd seen the eyes of death before.

Matt dialed 911 and handed me the phone. The voice at the other end of the phone line was calm and spoke with confidence. "Is your husband on the floor? If not, you'll have to move him so you can perform CPR."

"He's six-foot-four," I said. "I can't move him."

The voice was unwavering and calm, "Well, you just have to."

The robot in me took over, pushing the scene before me out of mind and turning off all feeling. I have had lots of experience with this and even though I know people have to do it from time to time in order to handle otherwise traumatizing events, in the long run it has not served me well.

"Matt," I said, "get hold of Dad under his arms and I'll take his legs. We need to move him to the floor." The floor he had just completed tiling. In a cumbersome maneuver we managed to move furniture, grab Dave and lower him to the floor.

CPR was useless. The voice inside my head was saying, in a high-pitched and futile scream, *nothing is going to revive him!* I knew if anything could bring him back it certainly was not going to be my desperate attempts at mouth-to-mouth resuscitation. I did it anyway, because—because that's what I needed to do—for Dave, for Matt, for me, for the hope against all odds that keeps human needs and wants living. Several times I spoke to him. Putting my face next to the side of his cheek I whispered into his ear. "Don't leave me," I said. But even as I spoke the words I knew it wouldn't help. Where was hope now? His blue eyes spoke back to me, 'I'm gone.'

All of this took only minutes to transpire and following the instructions of the invisible 911 operator was almost a relief. I can still hear Matt's voice breaking through to me as I continued CPR, "Mom, the paramedics are here. Mom, you have to move. Mom!"

Then a blur—I was kneeling next to Dave on the floor as I gazed up into the face of the policewoman who had arrived on the heels of our 911 call as she said, "You must leave the room while the paramedics see to your husband." A stream of police, paramedics, friends, my son and the coroner filled my tiny universe. I now realized I had put myself out of reach. My emotions were checked and my comprehension of the event was denied. Before leaving Dave with the paramedics, all I recall is repeating the same words over and over in an eventoned mantra. "What happened? What happened? I just don't understand what happened."

They moved into the room with their bags of equipment and monitors and walkie-talkies as I robotically moved outside to sit and wait. My intuition told me that he had had a heart attack. I have no idea how long the paramedics worked, but I remember overhearing one of them say to Matt, "It wouldn't have mattered if your dad was in a hospital when this happened. There isn't anything anyone could have done."

From the time the paramedics arrived and left, and the coroner came and left, I felt nothing. Nothing, that is, until the moment I found myself sitting outside with friends waiting for my son, Mike. He lived about an hour from our house and was on the road. The coroner had been alone with Dave in the house. I looked up and saw her come out of the house. She walked up to me and, with an arm outstretched, handed me Dave's wedding ring. I gasped and a deep breath of air filled my lungs in one gulp. For the first time since this awful scenario started to play itself out, I felt my loss.

I Have Seen the Eyes of Death Before

I have seen the eyes of death before
black rose, polished pearl, deep well

I have seen the eyes of death before
life abandoned, love gone, Earth left

I have seen the eyes of death before
retreated soul, free spirit, gates opened

I have seen the eyes of death before
treasure found, heaven won, peace eternal

I have seen the eyes of death before

Chapter II
The First Week

Once I would have said a memorable day was one with a happy event taking place, a day of joy. Now, to me, a memorable day is one when my heart has been touched so profoundly that memories are made. Good or bad. If I pause and think for a long moment, I have to admit to myself there have been other days over the years that created the iron and gold and the thorns and flowers of my life.

Our wedding day and the births of our children pop into my mind immediately, and there were goals accomplished. Also dreams not fulfilled. But the question looming before me was this—has this thorn in my life, which has brought such immense pain, brought some flowers along my path as well? And should I name them? Rose, lavender, peony, forget-me-not . . .

The next two weeks were filled with funeral arrangements and 'handling stuff.' The house was filled with friends, cards and plants. It was the stuff of life that propped me up to get on to the next task, the next day, and life. Don't think too much; just do the stuff. You know the stuff.

I met with our church pastor, Father John, to prepare the liturgy for Dave's mass and met with Roy from the mortuary. Roy. He and I were on a first-name basis. During the preceding twelve months he had handled services for both my mom and dad, and even for our daughter, Michele, seventeen years prior to the services that would be held to celebrate Dave's life. If anyone had ever told me that I'd be so intimate with a mortuary staff, I'd have told them they were nuts!

Perhaps because I did know Roy so well, I had no problem with our meeting as Mike, Matt and I sat in his office. I handed Dave's wedding ring to him and told him I wanted it placed back on Dave's wedding-ring finger. When Michele passed, I felt as though I'd made a mistake not letting her keep her birthstone ring. I wasn't going to make the same mistake with Dave's ring. Then I pulled a paper shopping bag onto my lap and pulled out a teddy bear. Roy's eyes grew large. I knew what he was thinking: 'What is this?'

"I'd also like you to put Dave's teddy bear with him." Roy did not skip a beat. He took the bear from me and excused himself as he left the room. A few minutes after he returned to our meeting, the intercom light on his phone lit up. He picked up the receiver and, after listening for a few seconds he said, "Yes, that's right, the teddy bear too." My sons and I gave each other a knowing look and smiled, repressing giggles at the thought of Dave's teddy bear and the reaction it must have caused with the mortuary staff.

Next, the cemetery.

There were good and memorable days to remember, even in the midst of all this sadness. There was laughter. There was life. Lizzie, Matt's girlfriend at the time, and I finally settled into working on the program for Dave's funeral service. She worked her magic on the computer laying out the text. Matt worked on scanning and laying out the back cover design, a great picture of Dave taken as he was walking away from my camera and alongside

Lake Louise in Canada with the magnificent mountains capped with snow and the lake in the background. Then the rush to Kinko's to run off all those color copies. We struggled with front to back and right side up to get the picture on the back centered. We laughed at ourselves trying to accomplish what should have been a simple task as we tried to get into some kind of orderly mass production.

Finally we got it, and when we were done we had another task to accomplish. Dave would have expected nothing less from me than doing some crazy creative cover for the program that would just be impossible, but wonderful. If anything gave my soul laughter and lightness it was pouring my creativity into something wonderful for Dave. I sat for hours contemplating the cover of this program. Finally it came to me. I wanted to emboss a Greek cross on the cover of all two hundred and fifty programs. Nuts, again! So, there we sat for hours embossing crosses, one by one, on each program. We laughed and talked about how Dave would think we were crazy as smiles spread across our faces. I knew he would have eventually approved and I loved every minute of the project. I made it a prayer for him. As I started to emboss each cross I prayed. *Be at peace.* When it was finished, I felt rather unsettled.

There, I was done with the stuff, right? Mind closed, heart wounded but still beating. I can't begin to understand how it happened, but air was still flowing in and out of my lungs even though I truly just wanted to be where Dave was. There was a part of me that sincerely believed that since he was gone I had no life or purpose, and I couldn't reconcile this feeling with why I was still alive.

Before I knew it, the day arrived for his services and I was standing outside the church doors being hugged and greeted by an ever-flowing line of friends, relatives and acquaintances. This was the same church where our children received First Holy Communion, where Michele and Mike were confirmed, where Michele's funeral was held and now Dave's. It seemed unfathomable to me that a building could be such a witness to a family's life from beginnings to endings, and I wasn't sure if I could stand to be there at that moment. My rational brain and my irrational heart kicked into gear. 'A church is more than a building,' I said to myself. 'It is people, and these people are our co-workers, friends and relatives.' Nevertheless, I paused when asked by someone many months later how I had the strength to greet all those people. To the casual eye it must have seemed unthinkable, as if I had some inner well of strength holding me up when, in fact, I wanted to hide. I wanted to run—far, far away, away from this day and its sadness and tragedy. And truth be told, I did hide for a while. I didn't want to greet all those people. I wanted to escape to somewhere, but there was no place to go.

I slowly walked into the church and made a feeble attempt to hide by leaning up against the back wall in a far corner. As I leaned against the wall, my inner voices played tug-of-war in my head: 'I can't talk to anyone right now. I want to hide' followed by, 'You can't just stay here, you need to go greet friends.'

Before either side had a chance to win, Father John, who would preside over Dave's service, came up to me and told me I needed to go outside to be ready to start the services at the back of the church where Dave was waiting. Of course I did. What had I been thinking? But then it started again—the long line and hugs.

It was not my hollow body and mind that gave me the strength I needed at that moment and throughout the day. Later, much later, I realized, if not for all those friends standing in that line I had dreaded, I would not have had strength to continue on that day, or any day for that matter. Friends, co-workers and family became my support, blessing and roses amidst the thorns.

Two of those roses were my very good friends, Paula and her husband, Dave. They offered to have a reception following Dave's services. Paula had created a beautiful sit-down lunch for all those who had come in support of my family. What I didn't realize until a few days later was, while she and Dave sat in the church watching people stream into the church, she started to get nervous about the huge number of people who were in attendance. "I had no idea you and Dave knew so many peo-ple," she told me. She began to wonder and worry about what she'd gotten herself into and how they were going to fit all those people into their home and feed them all. Fortunately, quite a few people had to return to work that day and only those closest to Dave, Mike, Matt and me came to the reception. The luncheon was beautiful and I wouldn't have survived the day without her.

While I stood in Paula's kitchen, I saw three people I didn't recognize. It turned out they worked for the same engineering company Dave worked for as a government contracts specialist, and one of them finally approached me and told me they were part of the team Dave managed in San Diego. They had traveled the 500 miles to Lafayette to be part of this day. I listened to them tell stories about how much they admired Dave and the way he managed his staff. It felt good to know others thought so highly of him and it eased me through the day— more blessings and roses.

In between all the preparations and for several weeks after, I wandered our house. I literally walked from room to room listening to the nothingness. To stop the pacing I forced myself to sit in a chair. I got up and wandered from room to room again until I thought I'd scream. On the inside I *was* screaming, 'HELP!' But there was no one there to hear me.

* * * *

The Sunday following Dave's services, I went to mass and sat on the same side of the church and in the same pew Dave and our children had sat during the many years of our involvement with this parish. Now I found it almost unbearable. I recalled a picture I have of Michele and Mike when they were small sitting on Dave's lap in the parish hall during a Christmas program. He was dressed like Saint Nicholas as, one-by-one, small children crawled up onto his lap while he listened to their dreams and Christmas wishes, gifting each child with a small candy cane. He had so much fun playing the role of St. Nick.

When was the last time I had gone to church alone? If anything pierced me like a sword, it was this first taste of how my life, in a matter of one week from the Sunday before, had changed. As I sat alone I thought, 'I'm back in this church again,' and I couldn't even find the words to pray. All I thought about was how much I already missed Dave and how it seemed an unfair lifetime since I'd seen my precious Michele. People were coming into the church and taking their places in other rows around me, but I was only aware of my hollow body sitting on this hard wooden bench—by myself. What do I thank God for? What do I ask Him for? Finally what I said, as I would find myself saying to Him for many years to come was, "You know what I need at this moment in my life better than I do. I have no words, no plan and no idea how I'm going to survive. So, I'm leaving it up to You."

After what seemed like an eternity, but was actually a couple of weeks of this futile existence of wandering and not knowing what to do, there was finally the moment of meltdown. Hiding from my great loss was no longer possible. He was gone and I was not, and wells of water from deep within me turned to sobbing until spent. There were no flowers in that moment and I was skirting around the issues at hand. Who am I? What do I do now? Does anybody care? Why am I here? Does it matter? All the who, what, whys I faced in the midst of thorns.

Deepest Shades of Black

Wandering from room to room
In some senseless attempt
To find an answer to this
Black and meaningless doom.

Who what why has snatched
My heart away with no warning
Leaving black on this sunny day
In May taking all of life away.

Life breath laughter and love
All fallen into shades of black
Leaving me alone lonely and
Waiting and wanting him back.

No other shades could be as black
As this part of me that no longer
Lives within my sight but only
In my heart from now to forever.

Chapter III
Reminders

I sat there staring into the palm of my hand at the round gold band thinned by years of wear. On a day in September 1967, it had signified all the hopes and dreams for the beginning of our new life together. Now its meaning was finality and it took my breath away. A new journey began, one I was not expecting, and one I did not want.

The inevitable questions loomed. What now? How do I go on without my life love and partner? These were huge questions with no easy answers, but one thing was crystal clear to me—my identity for thirty-eight years had been one of *couple*.

There were other identities as well like mother, daughter, and friend, but none was so all consuming as couple. How, after all these years, would I once again find an identity that said, *me*? The thing was, I didn't want a new identity. I struggled with everything that reminded me of the fact that I had no choice. Shouldn't I have a choice?

Over the following seven years I found there were plenty of choices to make, just no choice over the fact that I was now single. The situations that made me face this certainty were not subtle and wasted no time in shaking me into reality.

The government and financial institutions were the first to put me in my place, whether I liked it or not, and within a few short weeks they quickly straightened me out. Someone told me the first thing to do was to go to the bank and change the names on our bank accounts. So off I went. What did I know? Not much. I found myself to some degree following instructions and advice from my attorney, my financial advisor and 'whomever.' There were a lot of 'whomevers,' and one of them told me taking Dave's name off our bank accounts was some new Homeland Security issue.

Off to the bank I went feeling pretty confident and clear about what I needed to do and feeling emotionally prepared.

I sat with one of the bank's customer service employees and told him I needed to change names on our accounts. After some discussion, I ended up closing all our accounts and opening new accounts, which entailed completing and filling out new paperwork. I was up for anything, or so I thought.

Boxes, lots of boxes to check. My first choice was to check one of these boxes: 'Single' or 'Married.' I glanced at my left hand that tentatively held the new account form and saw my wedding ring. There was no box that said, 'Married in my heart.' Maybe that's what the 'Widow' box is for, but there wasn't one, and even if there had been I couldn't relate to that word. The dictionary defines a widow as:

> wid-ow (noun)
> 1. woman whose husband has died;
> 2. woman left behind;
> 3. short final line of a paragraph;
> 4. extra hand of cards

I couldn't even utter the word widow, but every definition fit exactly into the place my life had taken me and who I thought I had become—left behind, the final line of our lives, and the extra hand I'd been dealt. To identify with the word widow meant I had to confront my loss. I wasn't ready. But slowly my pen went to the 'Single' box and, against my heart's wishes, checked the box. I left the bank a little less sure of myself emotionally. I sat in the car with my head down as tears welled under closed eyes. Being so confronted with the black and white of my life brought the harsh reality back to me and I knew it was going to take some time to heal the raw wound I carried.

I collected myself and drove away from the bank comforting myself by thinking this ordeal was behind me and I wouldn't have to do it again. Wrong. Tax time arrived. I was now having a conversation with my tax accountant. He told me, "So, you'll need to change your W-4 at work and check the box that says, 'Head of Household.' " Okay, did I get a promotion or something? Done. I'm now the Head of Household. I held this again unwanted title until the day Matt was no longer my dependent and I found myself having to check boxes again. Now I was single again, but this time calloused enough to make the emotional pain bearable.

Right after hating the 'am I single or am I married' conundrum was being the odd person out. I can't say my married friends had stopped asking me for dinner or to join them socially, but being in a group and being the only one without a partner was so very strange and uncomfortable. The all-familiar things, both small and large, that made us a couple were gone. Dave's look from across a room at a dinner party, which might have been nothing more than eyes meeting for a second that spoke, 'I'm here;' the touch on my back as he passed behind me on his way to join the guys in the next room to watch football on TV; the glance that said, 'We have to get out of here before so-and-so drives me crazy.'

All the unspoken codes we shared were gone, and I couldn't shake the feelings of emptiness created by even these small gestures of being a couple. I had to remind myself that I had been married for thirty-eight years and that I shouldn't expect my feelings to change overnight.

Then came the fourth of June, just thirteen days after Dave's passing, a date that holds a special place in my heart. The evening started at 5:00 p.m. at a wedding I attended. I thought of every excuse possible to avoid this affair. 'People would understand if I didn't go,' I told myself. But in the end I had to go. The wedding was celebrated on the first hole of a golf course overlooking a picturesque scene of rolling hills, a pond and oak trees whose branches reached and arched as if trying to touch the green grass of the Earth.

Guests were starting to gather under a white canopy, so I took a seat at the end of a row and sat quietly trying to blend in or, better yet, become invisible. Sitting through this wedding was agonizing with words sounding so elusive and vows ending in forever and ever. From time to time I had to emotionally remove myself from the ceremony. It was just too difficult to bear and I closed my ears as if I was trying to close out sounds that seemed like fingernails on a blackboard.

The ceremony ended and I breathed a bit easier as we moved into the reception hall. I moved mechanically through the receiving line, found my assigned table and things were going smoothly.

I breathed a quiet sigh as I found myself sitting with family. 'Good,' I thought, 'I don't need to explain my actions to anyone or talk, chat or smile as if my mind wasn't a million miles away.' Then the band began to play and the dancing went on and on and words from a song kept running through my head.

Would you like to dance
under the moonlight,
hold me darling into the night.
Oh baby, do you wanna dance?

How did I put my feelings around this one? Yes, I wanted to dance, but it was another awkward moment. Other than dancing with my son, Matt, it wasn't working for me. One of the bride's relatives asked me to dance. I knew it was all in my head but my head was saying, 'Is this guy taking pity on me because Dave isn't here? Is everyone looking at me and thinking this guy asked me to dance because Dave's not here and I don't have anyone to dance with? The truth was, yes, and I'd better learn to get over it,' I told myself as I danced with him.

Then I was sitting at my assigned table again, and everyone at my table got up in unison, almost as if on cue, and headed to the dance floor. I sat alone and couldn't figure out which caused more discomfort, to dance or not to dance. My mind was tossed back to high school. Again, I was that young teenage girl sitting on the sidelines waiting for a dance partner, or prince charming, or someone. 'Socialize,' I told myself. I didn't have to have my dance card full. Once again I was having conversations with myself trying to rationalize the scene before me and trying to not have it hurt so much.

As the reception carried on, my cell phone rang and I was grateful for the interruption. (I know, very tacky, and normally I would have turned it off, but my daughter-in-law, Kristen, was due to give birth to my first grandson any day, so I made an exception.) The call was from my son, Mike, and he told me they were on their way to the hospital. I blissfully said my goodbyes. It was a relief to be leaving this gathering. I jumped in my car and within minutes I was on the freeway heading toward the hospital.

I sat in the hospital's waiting room for word that little Max had been born. Before the night was over, I held a swaddled bundle and looked into the eyes of my grandson. I was sure I felt Dave standing next to me. It would not be the last time I would feel Dave's presence and I thought about his last words on the anticipated birth of our grandson. The week before Dave's passing, he emailed me from work, "I am so weary. I just want to sit and hold our little grandson, but I guess I have to wait for that too." So, here was this little boy we were all waiting for. If only Dave could have waited thirteen more days before leaving. Now I would be Grama, only one half of a whole. Bitter, sweet joy.

Reminders of living without Dave were—and still are—everywhere, but they seemed especially pronounced during the first year of our separation. Even TV commercials showed no mercy. At that time a commercial was airing showing two couples, a young couple and an older couple, walking down a tree-lined path. Both couples are holding hands as they walk along, obviously enjoying their time to-gether. The younger couple is walking faster and passes the older couple. Then the woman of the younger couple turns her head and smiles at the older couple. The expression on her face says it all, 'Some day we are going to grow old and be just like you—together, holding hands.' Often I see this in real life as well, two people who (seemingly) have been together for years still caring for each other.

Watching couples walking hand-in-hand were not the only reminders that haunted me about Dave's absence. In northern California, where I have lived my entire life (other than three years when Dave was stationed in Massachusetts and Texas with the U.S. Army Security Agency) there is a mountain, Mt. Diablo, with a 3,864-foot summit. From our second-story master bedroom, I can view the mountain from either of two large picture win-dows. After Dave's passing, I once mentioned to Matt that I had a love-hate relationship with this mountain and he had nodded his head in under-standing and simply said, "Yeah." Dave was an avid bicyclist and on most weekends, barring rain, he would ride his custom-built Della Santa bicycle to the summit. At six-foot-four-inches tall, he found most bicycles didn't accommodate his long frame, but he loved this bicycle.

Not only can I view this mountain every single morning as I arise in the morning, but when I drive east on the freeway, which I do at least once a week, the mountain looms large. Every season has its way with the mountain. In spring, the gullies and ridgelines host all the greens of leaves, trees, bushes and grass; in summer, it bares the ochre yellows of wheat and dried grasses; in fall, rain clouds hover mid-point up the mountain giving it an ethereal and mystical ambiance; and in winter, there is even the occasional snow flurry which caps the summit in white. In all these seasons Dave would ride to the summit each weekend. Every time I see Mt. Diablo, the devil mountain, it brings a vivid image of Dave in his bicycling togs and his love of bicycling.

Several months after Dave passed, some of the friends he worked with called Matt and Mike and asked if they'd like to join them on a memorial ride for their dad up this mountain. To this day, every year, usually in May, these same co-workers host a ride in his memory. They talk about Dave, his sense of humor and working with him. Dave had swayed some of them into buying bicycles (some who didn't even know they wanted a bicycle!) and they would talk 'bicycle talk' about the Tour de France, or what ride they would tackle next. So, the mountain speaks to me of Dave, and my lack of understanding about how and why someone who was so fit could die suddenly of a heart attack.

In the case of the TV commercial, I used to turn the channel when I saw those couples. I would not be growing old with Dave and I struggled for days, no weeks, or maybe it was months with the concept of single or married. The mountain cannot be removed, so at some point in time what I finally realized was, at the core of who I am, being a couple will always be a part of me just as Dave will always be a part of me. Just as my parents had shaped me from childhood into adulthood, the years of our lives in our marriage had also, in no small way, made me who I am today.

Between Then and Now

My heart is in a constant goodbye
torn between then and now
the past not long enough and
the future unsure and faceless.

Reflections on this band of gold
a circle that would never end
beckons to a new life with all the
uncertainties of living and loving.

But there are no instructions
with this gold circle, only a promise
made long ago that love would be
forever and so it will be.

Only by this gold band and that
promise of forever love can this life
within me hope for a new beginning
of happiness new beginning of forevers.

Chapter IV
Ever Present

The difficult weeks that followed, one after another, did not go by quickly. It was as if time was being held at bay. Each moment seemed to elongate time and my surroundings seemed surreal no matter where I went or what I was doing.

I returned to my job with the company where I had worked for almost twenty years as a human resources specialist after only two weeks of leave. I figured I could be grief-stricken at work and at least have people around me; or, I could be grief-stricken at home and alone with only my fragile sense of life to envelop me, and that was definitely not an option. Staying home was also not much of a choice because wandering the house only presented me with walls of memory, not a secure sanctuary of peace.

I knew that, of all the places on Earth, work was not where I should be once I did return.

I lapsed into staring at the pile of paperwork that had amassed during my absence. I forgot passwords to programs on my computer and, worst of all, I didn't care. (Oh yes, I know—all signs of grief and depression.) I surprised myself by even summoning enough energy to get to work, but isn't that what automatic pilot is for? My emotions were checked at the front door and each workday just passed.

On that first day back to work, I turned on my computer and opened up Outlook to review the emails that had piled up during my absence. My heart skipped a beat—an email from Dave. I sat, frozen in time again and staring at the screen. Just seeing his name in that all-familiar format was startling. I read, *Time: Friday, May 20 at 3:30 p.m.* It was the Friday before he passed. *Subject: Leaving for Home.* I opened the email. Two simple words. That was the entire message. Two short, powerful, simple words —"Be Happy." In shocked silence, tears flowed down my cheeks while the words sent my spirit soaring with a somber kind of glee.

Here was a crystal clear message from Dave. His wish that I Be Happy.

That day's story doesn't end there. As if I wasn't going to take his message to heart, he sent me two more reminders that same day, just to make sure I 'got it.'

On that particular day, after putting in a day at work, I had been scheduled for a medical appointment at a local hospital. I had been diagnosed with multiple sclerosis in 2001, and when I am extremely stressed my symptoms start acting up. Needless to say, life couldn't have been more stressful than it was during those weeks. I wasn't surprised to find my vision compromised and my left leg weakened. One of the treatments to help relieve these symptoms is an infusion of steroids and my neurologist had arranged this appointment. While I was waiting in the lab, the technician asked me if I wanted to watch TV. The treatment would take about an hour and there were no other patients to chat with so I said, "Yes." Just as the picture came onto the screen a commercial appeared showing a banner that said—"Be Happy."

Okay, now I was getting a little unnerved. I drove home after my appointment, got out of the car, walked over to the mailbox and the top piece of mail was from Children's Hospital in Oakland, where our daughter, Michele, had many of her treatments for cancer. It was a promotional piece with pictures of children who were ill and undergoing treatment. Right across the bottom of the brochure were these two words—"Be Happy."

'So,' I thought to myself, 'now Michele has gotten into the act and was putting in her two cents' worth.' I had to smile. How could I turn my back on messages from two of the people I love most in the world? I am one of those people who believe that our loved ones on the other side communicate with us. I have no doubt who sent these comforting words to me because the coincidence was too much to ignore. Coincidences don't just happen and now these two little words—Be Happy—are carved in my heart and have carried me through some tough days and some major decisions as well. They have become a constant reminder, not only of Dave's wish for me and my life without him, but also a reminder of his absence.

Reminders are everywhere and continue as my life goes on while days, weeks and years slip between the then and the now. Some put a smile on my face while others do not, and one thing I know for sure is there's not enough I can say about some of the simplest things in life that can turn bad while one is grieving. I've talked to many who agree with me.

First, there's the grocery store. After accepting every invitation from friends to go to breakfast, grab a quick lunch or join them for dinner, the bathroom scale had started to tip higher and higher and there always comes a time when one must go to the grocery store.

Before I even got into my car to go to the store I realized I had a problem. I love to cook and Dave was my greatest fan and guinea pig. (But that's another whole tale to tell.) At first it was the place itself that I couldn't understand. I couldn't understand how all those people were just shopping and going on with life like nothing had happened. For some crazy, unrealistic reason I thought they should know the pain and heartache I was carrying.

As I pushed a grocery cart down one aisle and up the next, the same words kept repeating in my head, 'Stop the world, stop the world. I want out. I can't stay here.' I couldn't remember why I was there. Oh yes, I needed bread or something. I was buying for one instead of two so I couldn't even decide how much to buy. In the end, I just left with nothing because I decided I could manage with what I had at home—soup, an egg, whatever. I couldn't stay there one more minute. What I needed was not in that store.

The grocery store is also where you run into people you know and end up having conversations you don't want to have. They are all well meaning, and hey, they just want to know that you are doing fine. One day I found myself at the butcher counter ordering meat and spied someone Dave and I had known for years. He was not a close friend but was part of our community and I just couldn't speak to him. I had been on an emotional roller coaster all day and I just needed to be invisible, buy what I needed and leave. So I grabbed my meat order and found myself ducking down one aisle and then another making my way to the checkout counter so I could leave before I ran into him. It's a small neighborhood store. I zigged when I should have zagged and there he stood in front of my cart.

"So, you still living in the house?" he asked me. 'Okay,' I said to myself, 'that's not the worst question he could have asked.' "Yes, it's my home," I said. "Well, if anything every happens to either the Mrs. or me, we'd downsize." 'Good for you,' I thought to myself. I made polite conversation and retreated to my car to sit and take deep breaths. 'Be Happy,' I reminded myself. The roller coaster had to stop sometime.

More pleasant reminders surrounded me though, and I particularly remember my birthday only nine days after Dave passed. It was one of those 'non' days for me, and celebrating a birthday seemed irrelevant and unimportant. For weeks Dave had been asking me what I wanted for my birthday. I wasn't being very cooperative. I couldn't come up with anything because I thought I had everything I needed. I remember getting an email from him that read, "Really, you're not helping me. What do you want for your birthday—and I mean it!"

Then one day my cousin, Arlene, showed me a new toy she had received. It looked like a small digital camera but actually stored digital pictures. It was called a Magpics. So, I checked out the Magpics on the Internet and then sent Dave the Web address to the online store where they sold this little gizmo and then immediately forgot about it. Two days before my birthday, seven days after Dave passed, a UPS truck stopped in front of my house and the driver handed me a package addressed to Dave. I opened it and there was my birthday gift—the Magpics I had asked for. I looked at the order receipt and it was dated May 22. He had ordered it the morning of his passing.

The sun merely needs to rise in the morning for me to be reminded of Dave, and during the first months I seemed so aware of his presence. Whether this was because I was desperately looking for him to be in every little corner of my universe or not, I'll never know. Certainly even after all these long seven years, from time to time, I still see him driving his bright red Porsche, and every time I see a peloton of cyclists, I'm sure he's in the pack somewhere. Then there are specific events like the day I heard 'our song.'

Dave and I had planned a Mother's Day/birthday getaway for his mother to Yosemite. We had booked the reservations at the beautiful Ahwahnee lodge months and months in advance. Of course, things then took that unforeseen bend in the road, but I asked my mother-in-law if she would still like to go; and if so, I would take her. As it turned out she became ill and couldn't go, but my friend Paula went with me in her place. I can never pass up an opportunity to go to Yosemite. It was our favorite place on Earth. Dave and I tried to go there at least twice a year to drink in the natural beauty of the towering cliffs, cascading waterfalls and to be inspired by nature.

In the early morning of the day that Paula and I were heading to Yosemite, I was in my bedroom packing my suitcase and getting dressed to leave when I heard several chimes, almost like someone clinking a crystal goblet. Then quiet. Then a few more chimes. I realized it was music, a music box. Dave's music box. Quiet. Music. His music box sits on the nightstand next to his side of the bed and again, it played a few notes and stopped. I stood there staring at the box. Did I hear what I thought I heard? Then it started to play again. A few notes and stopped. Dave hadn't played that music box in years. I had given it to him as a twentieth anniversary gift and it played our song, *Close to You*. I found myself smiling and inside I felt a carefree lightness that had been missing. For me it was a sign from Dave and he was saying, "Go. Have a great time."

Was I viewing things with increased intensity because I was looking for signs, or because I had seen signs? It reminded me of a Bill Moyer presentation I once saw on TV. He asked the person he was interviewing how he could be sure there is a God. The guest said he believed there is a God. Could he prove it? Not scientifically. But, the guest seemed to believe that even if it is not true that there is a God, what harm had been done that he did believe? I believe these signs I see and hear and even dream are from Dave and every one supports me in the journey to be who I'm supposed to be on my own.

Along with all the sights and sounds, which bring the kind of happiness that lifts my spirits; or, the somber recollections of past and present, there are my dreams. I suppose, in a sense, these dreams have been a blessing because I have a friend whose husband passed just months after Dave and perhaps a year passed before she dreamt of her husband and it was agonizing for her. My dreams came in the ordinary and some not-so-ordinary variety. I have dreamed about Michele over the years, and it didn't take long after Dave's passing when I dreamt of him as well. When that first dream came, it was powerful. I've forgotten the particular life events surrounding me during that time and can't even recall if I was in the abyss or coming up for air. These two extremes seemed relentless as I tried to have a life. I must have been in the abyss though, because I really needed this dream. I remember so vividly that in this dream Dave simply came up to me, put his arms around me, hugged me and wouldn't let go. I was in ecstasy just feeling his arms surround me.

I wanted to stay there forever, but I woke abruptly with tears rolling down my face and for what seemed like minutes, but was actually only seconds, I could still feel the warmth of his hug. Powerful beyond words.

I had a conversation about a year ago with a professor at a local university who taught, among other things, dream analysis. I described this dream to him and also one I had a few years after Michele had passed. In this dream, I was sitting in our living room and she came running into the room. In my dream she was about ten years old and she was wearing a long red-and-white checked dress that she loved. She threw her arms around me and my face snuggled into her long strawberry-blond hair and I could smell the scent from the herbal shampoo I had used to wash her hair. After describing these two dreams to him he simply said, "Those weren't dreams. Dave and Michele were there visiting you." I do believe.

These two dreams were different than the day I walked through my front door, turned to go into the kitchen, looked up and saw Dave leaving the kitchen from the other end of the room.

This apparition mimicked the all-familiar nightly routine when Dave and I would have our evening chat and he would leave the kitchen to make his way to the backyard. His image was so real that I went to the doorway he had just passed through to see if he was still there. I wanted to follow him. I walked through the living room and the family room to the back sliding glass door hoping I'd find him watering the yard or sitting with his book reading. He was gone—again.

Thankfully, I still have my dreams of Dave. The vision of him only happened one time, but it is imprinted into my memory. I can have an instant replay whenever I need to feel his presence.

There Will Only Be One You

There will only be one you
one tall blue-eyed you
whose smile filled my heart
and arms enfolded me with
gentle silent strength and love.

There will only be one you
who won my heart in youth
opening and closing chapters
of life's journey from start to
end and then forever.

There will only be one you
as life sends me spinning
into uncharted realms alone
your presence ever felt will
soften life's sharp edge.

Chapter V
Here and Now

I know the way I feel today is not an overnight wonder. In the here and now, some six years after Dave's passing, I feel as if I can claim my life and claim who I am. That I have the right to Be Happy is as real to me as if I was newly born. If I measure, inch by inch, my life as I traveled in search of how and who I am without him, it is not one thing, not one person, not one prayer that has made the difference, but the many.

I'm not even sure I can go back in my memory to draw a straight line from there to here, which I now call my Earthly journey. What I do know is something inside me has changed. There was a day when I realized, and I mean really realized, that life is for the living. I had to find out exactly what that meant to me and pursue it. I needed to move with and toward tangible goals so I would truly be living my life and not sitting and watching the world act out around me. That meant moving out beyond the security of my front door. I started to look at security in a new light. Life changes and in trying to protect myself from the changes that had been thrust upon me, I was bound to isolate myself from living.

What was not so clear at the beginning of this journey, since I was living in a gray fog most of the time, but seems crystal clear now, is that by putting one foot in front of the other and moving, I was bound to get somewhere. One foot in front of the other. Small steps. And that 'somewhere?' I had no idea where or what that was. I shouldn't give the impression my life is now laid out before me and I have no questions to ask about the why of my universe. From time to time I still want to say, 'What the heck? What am I doing here, and why isn't Dave here?'

Sometimes, when I find myself a little too sure about the direction I'm moving, or when I'm having one of those bad days and need to realize how hard I've tried to find my life without Dave, I only have to go back and read some of my journal entries. Just a year ago I found myself writing the following, which clearly points to a day when nothing was crystal clear.

Journal Entry:
December 22

Is it the season? Is it the gloomy weather? Is it the five years of loneliness? How many times do I pull myself back from depression? It seems constant. Someone once said that being optimistic all the time is exhausting, and it is! There's a limit to what you can share with people— friends even. No man is an island? Sometimes I am an island. Emotions, confessions, personal enlightenment about self may not be subjects to share. These are the parts in my head that no one else can handle but me alone.

Ernest Hemingway made himself write five pages a day and I'm wondering if that would be single or double-spaced. I'll go with double spaced because I can't even write a paragraph on a day like today. I'm supposed to be writing my own story but . . . So who am I kidding? I have to laugh when people say, "You should write a book."

I find, among the problems of loneliness, is introspection. One would think that would be a good thing to do and I'm sure it has its place—like on a retreat geared toward self-enhancement or during a support process for those who might be trying to overcome an addiction to alcohol or drugs. But when it's about who I am as an individual, it's not so good as a steady diet. I know you (speaking to myself) don't want to hear this but today's study of self has brought you to what I am going to call the cliff of despondency.

Think the word is too dramatic? My contemplations, if that word seems more gentle than introspection, have made me realize that up until Dave's passing; and yes, I'm saying 'passing' although I've been told by a published author and screenplay writer that I should just come out and say, death— say it like it is, that one of the reasons I'm not progressing further in the process of healing (who came up with all the catch phrases?) is I find myself without purpose. There, I've said it. I know I do have one; we all have one— purpose I mean.

When I was a child, I remember a teacher saying our purpose as kids was to learn. We become educated, take jobs and perhaps get married and then our purpose, in the case of being employed, is to excel at our jobs. We might have joint goals with our spouses and work toward those and support our partner. We might have children and then our purpose is to raise our children the best way we can. So, basically I'm lost. What is my purpose?

This is reminding me of the poem I wrote in 2010 about a waterfall in Yosemite.

Yosemite Waterfall

The melted snow threw itself
from the precipice free-falling
to the valley floor below.

Its path prescribed, its
destiny a given, its purpose
unchanged, unchallenged.

Oh, such comfort, what pleasure
splashing, glinting in the sun, flying
carefree down the mountainside.

It did not wonder, did not struggle with
its existence, its purpose, its identity
for by its very nature it was perfect.

Why then should we—as much a
creation of God as melted snow
wonder ponder struggle for
our meaning purpose reason?

Well, we just do that's all.

My journal entry emphasized to me that, like everyone, I have bad days when I think I can't breathe and good days when I think things are swell. In the midst of all that though, I have reached a space of what I'll call—acceptance for now.

I sat on a bus a few months ago that was taking me and about forty other people to an art exhibit and had a conversation with the lady sitting next to me. I have known this woman for at least thirty years, but we hadn't seen each other in a long time and we were catching up with our lives and families as our conversation rolled around to our parents and aging. I told her about my ninety-six-year-old mother-in-law who has apologized to me from time to time for living so long. She didn't understand why God had left her here at such an old age. I knew why she was still here. She ministered to those around her with her optimism and graciousness. She was a role model for the elderly and on more than one occasion her caregivers have said they'd like to clone her. She's a ray of hope and cheerfulness among the aging and depressed. She had a purpose just like that waterfall. She was perfect just the way she was. She couldn't see her purpose even though I clearly could. Is it this way with all of us? Are we merely incapable of seeing the why of our being?

Although the answer to that question may elude me, I can usually find enough solace in the world to carry me through the grey days. Frequently, support and comfort comes to me in my dreams, as described in a journal entry I made in January 2007.

Journal Entry:
January 2007

. . . the sign I received last night in a dream from Dave was powerful. For some reason, I thought I was terminally ill and going to die. The dream was filled with people trying to take care of me. Then somehow I figured out it wasn't my time to die, but to live. I was in a huge crowd of people in a large hall of some kind. On the far side of the room with a sea of people between us, wearing a dazzling white shirt, Dave was jumping up and down with his arms stretched straight up yelling, "I love you." It was a powerful message that I must continue on, knowing I was loved.

The thread that got me from there to here started with the choices facing me and it was simply this: I had the choice of sitting at home and vegetating, wandering from room to room, or moving outside my small little realm past my front door. Along the way I realized that the flowers in my life would never bloom if I held on to the past.

Sacred Journey

The sun encompasses every soul
With warmth and daily sunlight.
If you're lucky enough to share
one truth will bear these fruits.

Our lives are not so different
Not really really different.
For every being upon this small Earth
Walks a path of life and death.

Our journeys have no one-way streets
Single smooth or rocky path.
But avenues filled with diversity
Joy sadness and test of spirit.

Listen to those around you
and you will be consoled.
For we are both blessing and blessed
When sharing our sacred journey.

Sweet Sixteen

Chapter VI
Sorting and Time

I was talking to a co-worker, a few years after Dave had passed, who had received a phone call around 11:30 p.m. the evening before. The call was from a friend whose son had been born with medical problems. Now, at four years of age he had died suddenly. With tears welling in her eyes, my co-worker told me of their conversation.

> My husband and I came home from the hospital and things were just as we had left them. Paul's toys sitting on the living room floor, his bedroom just as it was when we left. I wandered from room to room not knowing what to do. I couldn't, wouldn't or didn't want to pick up his toys. Didn't want to change things in his room. And then the inevitable. I just cried.

I knew exactly how she felt and other than wanting to jump into my car and drive right to their

house to hug them, it transported me to the morning Michele had passed.

She had been living more in the hospital than
at home. When she was home, there was an oxygen
tank sitting in our hallway delivering oxygen to her
night and day. Today, oxygen might be delivered
from a small tank with rolling wheels and a long
handle for pulling, almost like a traveling suitcase,
plug into a wall and would continually deliver oxygen. In those days, however, a truck drove up to our
house and the driver would wheel a five-foot-high
tank into our house on a dolly. The tank sat on a
square frame of wooden slats so it would not break
through the floor because of its weight. When the
tank became low we would call the medical supply
company and have them come to switch the tanks.

During the times she was home, Mike would
sleep in her room on the floor next to her bed to
keep her company and watch over her. She would
become indignant like any teenaged sister and throw
things at him—nothing heavy or wound-inflicting;
but I'm sure it was hard for him to handle. I knew
she was acting out her frustrations about being ill

and having her younger brother watch out for her. Secretly, I also knew it was because she loved him.

When she was at Children's Hospital in Oakland, she was surrounded by nurses who seemed to love having a teenager among their patients. She became the Pied Piper of the oncology floor. The little sick children would make their way to her room and climb up on her bed where she would tell them stories or do art projects with them. They always seemed to know when she had checked into the hospital. While Michele was in the hospital, Dave and I would take turns living there. This wasn't necessarily something sanctioned by the hospital but, for some reason, they seemed lenient with us while her pediatrician just shook his head in disbelief when he visited her. I stayed from Sunday night through Friday and Dave would come after work on Friday and stay until Sunday afternoon. It wasn't ideal, but on some level it worked.

The day before she passed, her doctors told Dave and me to go home and get some sleep. She had been in the ICU for several weeks and neither of us had really been able to get any rest. The attending doctor met me the next morning as I arrived at the hospital. He told me to call Dave and have him come immediately. Things were not looking good.

To this day, I do not recall when Dave arrived or if he made it there before Michele had to leave or not. Why I can't remember remains an uncomfortable mystery to me. Was I so out of touch with everything except Michele? I had put myself out of reach and on some level was blocking out the reality of the day. What I will never forget about this day was being alone with her when she passed and moving to the window in her room to say a prayer. As I stood staring out into the crystal-clear air, I felt a sensation in my chest as if an angel's wings were fluttering. I could feel it passing through me as if my daughter's spirit was saying a last goodbye. But, I know Dave did make it to the hospital because I also remember we made our way home together.

In the weeks that turned to months and then years, Dave and I were always there to support each other as we each took turns, or so it seemed, holding each other up in our sorrow. It was amazing to us that during the time Michele was in the hospital we witnessed many couples who crumbled under the weight of caring for their ill children. We were determined that this would not be our fate and that we would hold our little family together the best we could. Although I never consciously thought about where my emotional support would come from after Dave's passing, I realized I would have to turn to others to help me through.

Where my friend's story hits home was remembering how I felt when I went to Michele's closet for the first time and faced all her clothes, her diary, her jewel box, her everything that had been laid out quietly in her room, which then surrounded me, suffocating me with grief. Later that week, again alone, going through her things, I was struck by an overwhelming sense that I was sorting through her life. This was Michele. These things were her life, and I sat on the edge of her bed with my eyes fixed on my child's clothes, my hands gently stroking each item that she would never wear again. This was not the day I could part with her belongings. They would have to sit untouched until some other day when I could walk in her room and block out every thought in my head and every emotion in my heart. The delay was okay, because it had to be.

She loved art, was very creative and loved little kids. Even at her tender age of seventeen, I realize I had a lot to learn from her about how to love. Usually when she had to check into the hospital because her blood counts were too low, the nurses would scurry around moving patients to different rooms to try to secure a private room for her. She was usually the only older teenager on the floor, and, at seventeen, she might have even been considered an adult and the nurses tried to respect her feelings and privacy.

On one particular evening however, she was checked into a double room and was the roommate of a young girl who was suffering from the effects of sickle cell anemia. The little girl had been dropped off by a family member and was alone. She lay in her bed whimpering softly in an effort to deal with the pain that wracked her small body. Michele was in no shape to offer much comfort, but she tugged on Dave's arm and said, "Dad, help her."

Dave looked at Michele with a quizzical expression as if to say, 'If the doctors and nurses can't help her, how can I?' As if she was the only one who grasped the situation Michele said, "Hold her hand, Dad." Dave extended his hand and the little girl grabbed it and wouldn't let go.

After several weeks, I once again found my-self trying to clear out her closet and it was like trespassing on her life. Like the mom who couldn't move her little boy's toys, there were some things I would not part with. The clothes eventually were the easiest to give away. Her artwork and diary were an-other matter. I still have many of these things and I won't be letting go of these treasures. They are her very essence.

Seventeen years later, I reluctantly walked toward Dave's closet. I hadn't totally dealt with Michele's possessions and now I was facing Dave's. I opened the door and his scent washed over me and I thought, 'I can't do this,' and I shut the door.

At every turn reminders lived large. Large, like his red sports car sitting in the garage. Every time I opened that door the scents were of car oil, rubber bicycle tires and wood shavings. A twenty-foot canoe still hangs suspended from the garage ceiling. A boat Dave handcrafted. It dangles in front of me with constant reminders of being towed to a lake in the Sierras and pictures of the family making ready to paddle, paddle, paddle.

The car had to go. I couldn't bear being confronted by this small sports car he named 'Red,' into which he somehow managed to squeeze all of his six-feet-four-inches. I finally gave the car to Mike and Matt as a gift from their dad. It was theirs to keep or not. Unlike his closet, having my sons take the car away was a blessing. The closet door I could shut, but the garage wasn't as easily avoided.

Eventually, as in the case of Michele's clothes and shoes, one day I was able to open his closet and give away what I could. I started small and found it was easy to toss t-shirts and underclothes and that was all I accomplished when I once again shut the closet door, not to revisit it for at least a week. As in so many other aspects of moving through my grief, I was taking small steps. On many days I could only handle looking at Dave's possessions in increments of ten or fifteen minutes, but I allowed myself permission to stop when I couldn't face the task any longer. In the end, all I kept was his Army uniform and his wedding trousseau jacket (do you call men's wedding clothes a trousseau?). And, I must admit, after seven years, all his ties are still hanging from his tie rack and his bookcase still holds his favorite reads. These remaining items seem to capture his spirit, are a comfort of sorts and are not up for disposal; and, I am okay with that.

Eventually all this sorting of clothes and possessions narrowed like a wide rushing river into a small creek where the water trickled peacefully. Then I found time became an even greater equalizer. I recall asking a friend, "Do you know the phrase, *time heals?*" His face lit up with what might have been anticipation that I'd say I was healed, and he said, "Yes!"

"Well," I said. "They lied." I often feel bad about having put him in such an unpleasant situation and his face said it all. His wide-open grin turned to a frown and I realized it had been unfair to ask

a question and quote a saying I so adamantly dis-
believed.

I know the adage is old. *Time heals.* It seems
like such an easy phrase gently flowing from the lips
as one attempts to help, to say something that will
give comfort. I could sense when this phrase was
going to be uttered by a well-meaning acquaintance
and my insides would immediately bristle. There is
some truth to the phrase, but it's not the whole truth
for me. The wound that pierced my body and soul is
still very much alive, and I dare say, always will be.
For me, time did not heal. Time passed and my life
changed.

Every evening upon arriving home after
work, Dave would meet me at the front door with a
kiss and a glass of wine. We'd move around the
kitchen in a kind of comfortable waltz as I prepared
to make dinner and he, my partner, listened to me
and also shared his day. Mostly, in those last days,
I vented because I had been caring for my parents
and frequently I would stop at their house on my
way home from work to make sure they had been
taking their medication or to drop off groceries.

After hearing about how things were going with Mom and Dad, Dave would gingerly and slowly make his way to the far end of the kitchen and disappear through the doorway, (the same doorway, by the way, that I saw him pass through several weeks after his passing) partly wanting to hear what I had to share and partly not; and, he would make his way to the backyard with a copy of *Bicycling* magazine or the latest novel he was reading. He'd water the yard and read with his cocktail. I would make it outdoors with an appetizer, maybe a little cheese or nuts to tide him over while I cooked dinner. He would often be my guinea pig for a new recipe I was testing.

Simple acts during ordinary days. These are the routine acts that time heals. Each day after Dave passed, probably for weeks, I'd walk through our front door and Dave was not there for our routine waltz. Eventually, the routine changed. I can't call this 'healing.' I call this 'change' because I still miss our evening time together, but now I don't expect it.

My mother once told me she tried not to expect too much because that way she wouldn't be disappointed when things didn't work out the way she would wish or dream. I found this very sad but, on another level, so very wise. I realize, to a great extent, she was protecting herself from pain, both from what she wished would happen and what she knew wouldn't happen. I found myself adopting her philosophy. If I didn't expect Dave to be there in the evening, I couldn't be disappointed. At first this worked on a superficial level and one day it was so. For me this wasn't complete healing. It was a life change the hard way and total acceptance still wasn't part of the deal.

Sorting and Time

There is a timing to this life
we each must travel solo.
Some for staying in the now
some for moving forward.

Can't clean his closet this month
Nor move his favorite books.
Can't give away her dolls today
maybe never will.

No rules to say I'm moving fast
Or going way too slow.
There is a pace in my heart
That asks for rhythmic flow.

Don't be in such a hurry
To make this disappear.
For on some morning someday
There will once again be cheer.

Chapter VII
Touch
(and Bear Hugs)

One of the greatest things I miss about Dave's absence is touch, and part of that list includes the bear hug. Bears play a not-so-small role in our family. At last count there were over a hundred bears that have graced our home over time. Each was named, and each one had its own story.

As is the case with most children, our children received bears from grandparents and from Dave and me as birthday or Christmas gifts starting with a small wheat-colored cutie with moving arms, legs and head that Dave gave to Michele on the day she was born called *Ted*. She would carry this little bear around by its ear when she first learned to walk and hugged and loved it into her teens when it then sat on her bed. Ted now sits on a top shelf in my den with one ear hanging on by threads, one arm that has fallen off, its movable neck weakened by constant holding that now tilts to one side, and its black thread nose partially missing from the gnawing it received from our teething toddler. Michele also received a lot of bears from friends and family while she fought cancer.

Along with all the critters that Michele, Mike and Matt amassed, Dave was like a little kid when it came to stuffed bears. Each time we visited a national park, he would buy a local bear for me. To this day, three bears sit in the back seat of my car safely belted in—*Ahwahnee, Yellowstone* and *Tahoe*. And of course, he had his own bear—*Falkland* (which was laid to rest with him); as I have mine, *Timothy*. Timothy still sits in my bedroom keeping watch over me. We all loved our bears.

The story of our bears is not meant to make light of, belittle or skirt around the issue of the very profound and real loss of intimacy I suffered when I lost Dave.

For the first three nights after Dave passed, I slept on the family room sofa. Then I realized that I wasn't getting the best rest and that I had enough to handle emotionally, without lack of sleep to complicate my life even further. I recall walking up the stairs to our master bedroom on that first night when sleeping on the sofa was no longer an option. My body felt heavy with the weight of grief as I took each step slowly and tentatively, almost as if I was afraid of what I would find when I reached the top landing and walked into the bedroom. What I found was nothing, or should I say, no one; and that was the problem.

I woke each morning looking at his pillow. It lay there flat and smooth and it hadn't been punched into a comfy mound to support his head. A king-size bed can be a gulf—a gulf with no one on the other side. There was no escaping the need for sleep however, and each evening, no matter how well I managed emotionally throughout a particular day, at the end of the day I had to sleep, and I had to sleep in our bed.

Some nights found me so exhausted emotionally and physically that I fell asleep as soon as my head hit the pillow. Other nights, I'd pull Timothy into my arms and weep. Falling apart makes a lot of noise. Alone. All alone—my bear and me.

The noise of falling apart wasn't just in all the tears and weeping. Noise was also found in emotional pain, the constant battle within myself trying to figure out how I was going to survive without Dave's hugs or touch or love and still wear a face that said, 'I'm doing just fine.'

There was also the pain of the lost routine Dave and I shared each morning as we both headed off to our jobs—a kiss and, 'Have a nice day.' Another part of my life was missing, and this loss became more pronounced when I returned to work after my all too short two-week leave.

The 'waltzing' time in the evening when I returned from work and he met me at the front door with a glass of wine was always accompanied with a hug. Depending on how his day had been or how my day had passed it would somehow, without a word from either of us, be explained by the length of our hug. Bear hugs, which lasted a pretty long time, usually meant there would be a lot of sharing to do that evening on the back patio over a glass of wine and hors' d'oeuvres. I have to admit there were a few times while caring for my parents when Dave and I stood clinched in an embrace I wasn't readily willing to give up too quickly until one day Dave just said, "Break!" I had to give it up—and we stood there laughing.

There was no easy way out of healing the hole left in my heart that ached for Dave, and it would be the sweet tide of memories that would carry me through and move me forward.

One of my fondest memories of Dave's caring love took place at Lake Louise in Canada while we traveled for ten days visiting all the national park lodges from the Ahwahnee in Yosemite, California, up into Canada to Chateau Lake Louise and returning home via Paradise Inn on Mt. Rainer in Washington, Timberline Lodge on Mt. Hood in Oregon and Crater Lake Lodge in Oregon.

We had just finished a hike around Lake Louise and up into the mountainside on our way to discover The Lake Agnes Tea House, originally built in 1901 by the Canadian Pacific Railway as a refuge for hikers, which started serving tea in 1905. It was a fatiguing three-and-a-half mile trek with a climb up to an elevation near 6,700 feet. Every time we came to a bend in the narrow, craggy path Dave would ask if I wanted to turn back. A few times I almost gave up, especially when I found us hugging the mountainside and gingerly walking sideways because the path was so narrow it was the only way to continue without sliding down the mountain. But, we persevered because the tea house might be just around the next bend and we would miss out on stopping for soup, bread and a cup of coffee or hot cider if we gave into the rigorous climb. On we pushed—and we pushed ourselves physically. We finally reached our goal and it was well worth the trip, but by the time we got back to the lodge, we were both physically hurting. I mean—'Don't ask me to move another muscle and pass me the Advil kind of hurting.'

Earlier in the day we had browsed a local bookstore and purchased a children's book about bears and Lake Louise entitled, *The Snowbears of Lake Louise*, by David Chesky. It was another of our favorite rituals, to purchase a children's book whenever we traveled to a new destination—a habit I have continued over the years.

As we both sat in our room, trying not to move a muscle, Dave picked up the book and said, "Come over here and sit with me, lean back and put your legs across my lap, close your eyes and rest. I'm going to read to you." At first I balked, "Read to me? Of all the crazy . . ."

"No," he said. "It will be relaxing and you need to relax." I sat there with my eyes closed, legs draped over his as he read to me and rubbed the aching muscles in my legs. The last time someone had read a children's book to me, I was a child myself. It was the thoughtfulness of this otherwise simple act that will always remind me of why I loved this man.

The story, by the way, was about an old couple who went skiing, became trapped and had thought for sure they would die as they became covered in new-fallen snow. The Lake Louise bears gave them herbal tea that worked magic and made them young again. At the time, I just wanted my muscles to stop hurting, but now it seems like an appropriate story—to be young and together.

Fortunately, I still have my family and friends who give that needed hug, who lend an ear of understanding; but even after seven years, it is hard not to have the loving touch of someone who really cares in a more personal kind of way, the bear hug that says, "I understand," the thoughtfulness that speaks volumes about sharing life together. Memories carry me through quietly.

Speaking of Love

Words are an unnecessary intrusion
When love is spoken in quiet supplication.

More than your warm hands softly
Soothing away the cares of a day
Touch transcends time and space
Speaking through a gentle hug.

A tilted head and gleam in your eye
Talks so sweetly of fond and helpless love
Their words fall on my heart, I see your
Inner beauty they utter tenderly.

An offering of spring flowers and my nose
Is intoxicated with the delicious scent.
Reminders that beautiful blooms will fade
But not the everlasting blush of love.

A song, a poem when shared by two
As it gently caresses the ear in unity
Bonds two spirits, two souls becoming
Romantic language forever ours.

Two lips meet and impart the heavy
Taste of love and filled my being with
Only you and the world disappeared
Until life crashed in around us.

Words are an unnecessary intrusion
When love is spoken in quiet supplication.

Chapter VIII
Past My Front Door

Although I started my new journey the moment I knelt next to Dave on that tile floor and whispered goodbye, within a year I had to take a hard look at my future. For the next four years I found my suitcase both inside and outside my front door. It was hard to press into my new life, but I kept trying new roads. Like walking a labyrinth, I opened my heart and hoped it would lead me to a new sacred place.

Once I got back to my full-time job, my time was consumed with the ordinary daily grind. The first weeks back at work reminded me, in a sense, of going to that grocery store. Driving thirty minutes, walking the few blocks from my parked car in the middle of Oakland's busy downtown financial district to the high-rise building in which I worked, and taking the elevator to the twentieth floor, left me impressed with the coldness of a city built of cement, tar, steel and glass. After returning home one evening I sat on my backyard deck and gazed at the oak tree-covered hilltop on the other side of the valley. I breathed deeply to relax the tension in my shoulders and even though I knew it was financially impossible for me to leave my job now, I knew neither my job nor the big city could heal me. It would be another three years before I found myself leaving full-time work.

The City

Into the afternoon sun
Tall monuments surround
Empty space overwhelms
Lonely and isolated realm

Cold and straight and grey
Cement and glass reign
This world is not real
Its hardness cannot heal

Unforgiving and softless
Echoes haunt with hardness
The soul, heart and being
Alone and longing

The weekday early rising, commute traffic, work, more commute traffic, a glass of wine and an evening of reading or television or catching up on correspondence and emails only helped to fill the hours of a day. Weekends proved a challenge at first, but I tried hard to fill them with activities as well. My goal pointedly tossed me onto a path of ignoring Dave's absence. The more activities that kept me engaged, the better.

After Dave's passing I almost immediately called my cousin, Arlene, who had lost her husband at the age of forty-nine, ten years younger than Dave. Her story mirrors mine in many ways and we talked about how unlikely it was for two cousins to befall the same loss. One day we went to an art exhibit at St. Mary's College in Moraga. After seeing the exhibit, we wandered the beautiful campus and found seats in a small courtyard that surrounded a set of side doors leading into the campus chapel— the chapel where Dave and I were married. I sat on the bench, my head swaying slightly back and forth as an awareness settled over me. My world would always hold constant reminders of my life with

Dave, especially since we both grew up in this area. Over the course of our thirty-eight-year marriage, we rarely ventured far from our childhood homes in the San Francisco East Bay.

As my cousin and I talked, our conversation turned to the many women who had lost husbands as we had at an age too young and we tried to figure out how we could reach out to them, how we could touch each others' lives, how we could move on with our own lives. Some pretty unlikely ideas came from our conversation while we sat in the afternoon sunlight that shouted life into my ears. How many times had someone said to me, "You need to write a book?" Oh, we came up with some pretty funny ideas, like the book we'd write entitled, *One Hundred Cheap Ways for a Widow to Spend an Afternoon.* Over the course of these years, Arlene has become one of the roses in my life as both a steady and understanding support and a kindred spirit. This outing marked the first step past my front door and into a journey that would not allow me to turn back.

I love lists. I'd even call myself a great list maker. Depending on the seriousness of a subject,

I can make a list of the same information on a piece of ordinary paper, then on graph paper, then put it into a computer spreadsheet and even make a special folder for it. The seriousness of the list I was about to make, however, would take me to new heights as I created it over and over again in the years that followed.

I know it's a bit over-the-top, but I had to collect my thoughts and get some order into my life and this was one of my many attempts at order—or was it procrastination? As long as I was writing a list, I was doing something about my life, right? Whenever life handed me more than seemed feasible to balance, Dave had always said, "Just stay organized." Whatever the real role lists play in my life, they do have a place in my journey and this list started recalling the activities and interests that were at my very core, the interests that took a backseat years ago before taking on the role of wife, and then mother and raising a family.

On one of those afternoons, when I found myself wandering from room to room, I mentioned to my son, Matt, that I was making a list of all the things I wanted to do; but, I admitted I couldn't seem to move myself past the 'list phase.' He walked up behind me gently placing his hands on my shoulders and slowly moved me toward our piano that sat in a corner. "Start here," he said. "Play the piano. It's just sitting here not being used." He was right, and I would find it usually took someone on the outside looking in on my world to move me to accomplish what should have been obvious to me, but never was.

Before the month was over, I had contacted the local music shop where all my children had learned to play instruments during their elementary school years. One of the piano teachers, Carol, had a late afternoon slot open. I took it and, after work once a week for forty-five minutes, a new routine entered my life. After a year of lessons, the piano that sat in the corner of my living room had a new life. It was a small step, but it was the start of creating new avenues. I had to practice and I had homework to complete in the very same music workbooks I had used as a child. I was learning again and I don't know why it surprised me when I realized it was so simple to move my energy from the list to picking up the phone and making that first call to the music shop.

My time with Carol, though only forty-five minutes each week, introduced me to a new person who shared her love of music with me. We talked from time to time about her students, mostly grade school children, and about a recital she was planning. I asked about a recital for her handful of adult students, but she admitted it was a little harder to make that happen. Within a month, the baby grand piano that my son once reminded me was just sitting there not being used was now surrounded by five women taking turns listening to each other play. Music makes me happy and it lifted my spirits to realize how easy it was to take a step past my front door to make things happen around me.

As the women left and I cleared the dishes from dessert and coffee, I wore the grin of contentment after sharing an evening with new acquaintances. I settled into my chair to savor the evening, but the pleasure of just a few hours before slipped away and the dark cloud of loneliness, which had been abandoned for a few precious, enjoyable hours, once again settled over me. I was alone again.

Happier Pursuits

Yes, first I will go and go until there is
no time left unattended nor unscheduled solitude.
This will surely bring some peace to
my weary heart, some calm to this frantic search.

Though not intended these escapes have changed
their meaning and become part of who I am.
These outings have given me new interests
and a new vision of why God has left me here.

And so my life has a new direction and
A changed view of all the living within reach.
Every outing has fed my soul
And turned my days to happier pursuits.

Chapter IX
Mostly 'Ordinary' Happens

Most of my days have not been of the *extraordinary* kind. For the most part, my life has been filled with ordinary days. But even in the ordinary, I still faced living without Dave. These ordinary days were not the Earth-shaking kind, thank goodness, like the day Dave passed, the day of his funeral or even the days of wandering the house and weeping tears of pain and loss.

Ordinary days were more like the grocery store day, or just the time spent with the mundane stuff of life, like cleaning the house, feeding my Koi fish in a pond in my yard, doing laundry and watering my garden.

What seems so interesting to me now is all the ways I had to adapt to the many things I found myself having to tackle, fix, repair or deal with that had been accomplished by Dave, or both of us as a team.

I never gave much thought about how much work it took to run a household. I mean—I had my jobs inside and Dave had his jobs outside—with a few overlapping chores we did together. But handling the whole of everything—alone? Once again I heard Dave whisper in my ear, 'Just stay organized.' I found it took more than organization to handle maintaining house and home and I failed a lot along the way.

First there was the garden. How was I to know there were four separate sprinkler systems out there?! Actually, if I think long and hard about it, I did know, but never really gave it much thought. 'You can do this.' I told myself. All I had to do was turn on one sprinkler system at a time and continue until all four of the sprinklers had their thirty minutes of watering time. (Due to our low water pressure, I could only turn on one set of sprinklers at a time.) I would get home from work at 6:00 p.m. and finish watering by 8:00 p.m. Piece of cake! Why did I distinctly remember Dave sitting out on the back deck relaxing and reading while the backyard sprinklers were running? I can't seem to do that. Then I remembered—I was inside making hors' d'oeuvres and cooking dinner. (No complaining here—it's what I loved to do—cook.) Now I was getting the watering done, but I couldn't manage the sitting down and relaxing part.

A year had passed when I found the daisy bush had died. I was supposed to prune the rose bushes back in January and since that didn't happen the bushes were stretching their twiggy arms every which way—plus there were a few dead ones, too. Dave must have been shaking his head in disbelief. This whole watering, outside thing was taking more planning than I could ever have imagined. Forget about all the potted herbs Dave used to plant for me each year. That wasn't happening. I was determined this wasn't going to get the best of me. I would persevere and I hoped it would all find an orderly way of being handled before all the plants gave up on me. Over the years, I've grown to love winter and its automatic watering system provided by nature's rain.

Then I realized the wooden decks needed re-sealing, but I couldn't deal with that. It would have to wait until I got the gardening thing under control.

I had many phone conversations with my friend Linda, as we both tried to encourage and push ourselves to undertake a myriad of tasks on our own without Roy and Dave. (Linda's husband, Roy, passed just five months after Dave.) One day a plan took shape. We need to make a list, we agreed. Oh no—not another list. The idea was—every time we managed to handle a project or tackle something on our own that hadn't been our job, we would write it down on our 'I Can Do This' list. No task was too small to make it onto the list. If taking the garbage bins to the curb once a week to be collected was a task the guys would have done, then it would make the list once we had handled it on our own. Granted, moving garbage bins to the curb is not a monumental feat—they do have wheels. There were, however, a lot of other tasks that came up as a homeowner, car owner and just citizen-at-large, that were not as simple as the garbage bin task.

One day I was preparing to take a shower. I pulled out the knob in the shower that turned on the water and I was startled when the entire part came off in my hand. I stood staring at the knob wondering how I was going to fix it. I looked at the shower wall where the knob had been attached and saw a metal post. I went to the garage and found a pair of pliers. For six months I used this tool to pull the post out of the wall to turn on the water. I told myself that on some level it was a fix, but I was embarrassed for myself. I couldn't tell Mike and Matt. It would be an admission of failure not to be able to handle the simplest of tasks.

Eventually, one morning, I just decided it couldn't be that difficult to fix. I was tired of using the pliers and because of the angle I had to put my body in in order to pull the post out, my back was starting to hurt. Well, this was ridiculous. How hard could this be? I made my way to our local hardware store, knob in hand, and approached a salesperson to ask for some direction.

I left the store with a new knob and full instructions about the necessary fix. All it took was a screwdriver and one screw to replace the part. It was so easy. I felt a little foolish for not having tackled this task months sooner. This made the list—'one repaired shower knob.'

Then there was the day my cousin, Arlene, and I were heading out to have lunch with our Aunt Jessie. As I drove my car along the freeway, a shrill beep escaped from my car dashboard. A cartoon picture of an oil lamp was flashing relentlessly. OIL it was screaming. I panicked! Do I pull off the road? Do I ignore it and just keep driving? Am I going to do irreparable damage to my car? My head was spinning! Fortunately, Arlene was already familiar with handling car problems.

"We just need to go to a gas station, buy some oil and put it in," she said calmly. Okay, that seemed easy enough, but I didn't even know where to PUT the oil. "Not to worry," she said. It's so nice when someone else is staying cool, calm and collected when I'm about ready to blow a gasket. We bought the oil, found the oil well and added oil and all was good. Now, of course, I've added oil to the car numerous times—in fact, I'm a pro at it. But it took time to learn. I put that on the list of things, 'I can do.' Some tasks made the list but were not as easy as using tools or adding oil to my car. They were challenges in life and they made the list in CAPITOL letters.

Unlike broken faucets or car problems, caring for Dave's mother while still finding my path in life became both a loving distraction and a huge responsibility. I had cared for both my parents as they aged and became frail. Fortunately, I still had Dave's support while caring for them. But my mother passed just four months before Dave, and while he was there to help me grieve this great loss, my heart did not have time to heal before having to face Dave's passing. When Dave died, he left his mother when she was ninety-two years old. Since Dave was an only child and his only aunt and uncle, both deceased, had never married, he had no siblings or cousins. This left her care squarely on my shoulders while I was still working full-time.

Everyone, including my friends, called her *Grams*. She lived alone in her beautiful four-story home in the hills of Berkeley. She was very independent and drove her car until she failed her written driver's test when she was about to turn ninety-three years old. I sold the car because she was driving it occasionally with no license, and she didn't quite get the ramifications if she drove without a license and had an accident.

All went along pretty smoothly until the day I got a phone call from one of her friends telling me she hadn't been able to reach her by phone. I hopped in my car and made the thirty-minute ride to her house. I used my house key to let myself into the house and called her name. I had no idea what to expect or where she was. Unlike the day I was unpacking groceries and wasn't thinking the worst, this time the worst did enter my mind. 'Please God, don't let me find her unconscious or worse,' I prayed. I tentatively walked further into the house and called to her again. In response I heard a faint voice calling my name. She was in her bedroom on the second floor of her home. I raced down one flight of steps, entered her bedroom and found her on the floor. She had slipped out of bed and had been on the floor, unable to get up or reach her phone for almost two hours.

This was the beginning of the end of her independent living, and shortly thereafter I had a talk with her about looking into assisted-living accommodations. Arrangements had been made for her to spend a week visiting her accommodation of choice, Mercy Center in Oakland, operated and maintained by a Catholic order of nuns, the Sisters of Mercy. It was a wonderful environment, both in the staff that worked there and the facility itself.

When the day came for me to pick her up, she sat in her living room with her feet up on a stool and said, "I'm not going." This would make the third time we had made these arrangements and she had backed down, refusing to go. I totally understood—this was her home and she was giving up her independence, but I also knew she couldn't live there and take care of herself. I tried to reason with her, "What if you fall again and injure yourself, or worse?" I asked. "So what?" she would say. "I'm old and I've lived a wonderful life and I don't know why God still wants me here anyway."

This time had to be different. I knew I had to make a decision about her living accommodations and it was stabbing me in the heart to push her. I had to call in my backup troops, someone with the calm of reason. While the two of us sat in her living room at an impasse, I called Mike. If she'd listen to anyone it would be one of her grandsons.

"Mike, Grams won't go," I said.

"Let me talk with her," he said. I passed the phone to her and watched as she listened intently to what her grandson had to say, and then a tear welled in her eye as she choked back a tear. She hung up the phone and handed it back to me and said, "Okay, I'll go." To this day I don't know what Mike said to her, but whatever it was, she succumbed to our wishes.

That wasn't quite the end of the story, though. Mike came to her house and the three of us made our way to Mercy Center together. We checked out her apartment, completed paperwork and chatted with Sister Carmen about the meal schedules, activities and daily mass, and then walked the grounds with her. Sister Carmen invited Mike and me to join Grams for lunch before leaving.

The three of us sat at a lovely table in the dining room with other residents. Everyone was very friendly and accommodating, but the three of us sat there unable to eat. We had no appetite as we all faced what this day meant for Dave's mom. I observed my mother-in-law staring at her food with her head slightly bent down as she whispered in a quiet voice, "This is the hardest thing I've ever had to do." My heart was breaking for her and I could only imagine how difficult this was for her to face. I didn't want to leave her, but the time came when we had to make our way home and Grams had a new life to begin.

Time would verify that making the move had been the right thing for her and it left me in the unenviable position of having to sell the home she had lived in for some forty years. It was a monumental task to liquidate a four-story home that held many family heirlooms. She, however, had left her home and never looked back. She simply knew I would handle everything and I worked to add this new task to my list of things, 'I can do.'

One afternoon as I worked through the house sorting and clearing, I took a break to eat lunch. I pulled a chair out onto the balcony that takes in a panoramic view of the San Francisco Bay and the Bay Area bridges. I recalled all the beautiful sunsets our family had witnessed from her living room and this balcony over the years; each sunset different, each one more beautiful than the last. I was overwhelmed with the sense I was clearing, once again, the life and the memories of a loved one. Even though Grams was very much alive and doing well for her age, I was left with this huge responsibility. I looked out past the Golden Gate Bridge and said out loud so he could hear me, "Dave, you should be here helping me!"

Many times I still had difficulty tackling each new task as it came along. Occasionally, when things popped up in twos and threes I would feel depleted and struggled to pull myself back together—one more time. It was exhausting. There never seemed to be an end of things to learn, things to handle.

What I know about all this learning and all the things that made it onto the, 'I can do this list,' is there was generally someone by my side to help me over each little and big hurdle—whether it was a friend, a family member, or a friendly salesperson at the hardware store. Even though much of the time I thought I was totally alone, the reality was, in a very real and relevant way—someone else was always there too.

Sometimes that someone was Dave, and his presence showed up in a host of unexpected ways that gave me pause for thought and bolstered my spirit to continue on.

> Journal Entry:
> September 2012
>
> What I love best about all the poetry books Dave has given me over the years is the handwritten inscription he wrote in each one and also noting the particular occasion and year. He knew of my love for poetry in all its forms. Today, I went to my shelves of poetry and grabbed a book I had forgotten all about. He had given it to me for my birthday in 1983. The inscription reads: 'You are my music (Three-Quarters Time). You are my love. Happy Birthday.'
>
> 'Three-Quarters Time? That's not even a whole,' I thought to myself. 'I wonder why he wrote that sentiment?'
>
> The book of poetry is entitled, *Those Who Ride The Night Winds*, by

Nikki Giovanni. I sat flipping pages through the book and randomly stopping to read some of the poems. One particular title jumped off the page. I had found the reference to Dave's inscription, and as I read it I realized it was about dancing and music and how we fit into the rhythm of each other's lives—like our waltzing time in the kitchen after a day of work.

Question answered. Three-quarters time—a dance. How did you forget this lovely sentiment? Perhaps its purpose was for you to find it today and bolster you up as you greet the ordinary days. It could be sad too, if I let myself go there . . . once again realizing my great loss. But today it is just an affirmation—keep going—I love you still.

There were enough ordinary days that made me face my great loss, so reading this book inscription was like taking a breather.

I recall one afternoon when I took Grams for an outing. We had been invited for lunch at the home of my daughter-in-law's parents who lived about an hour away. They were both so supportive of me after Dave passed and Grams had always enjoyed their company.

After a wonderful visit we began our drive traveling south on Highway 101 heading for home, me to my house and Grams to Mercy Center. The scenery was beautiful with rolling green hills and sunny skies. Grams was just happy to be out on the road and away from the confines of her little two-room apartment. I made a comment as we drove about having to pay attention and not wanting to miss our exit and possibly getting lost. I didn't want her to become concerned so I added, "We have all the time in the world if we get lost. So don't worry." Then came her reply:

"That's right. We have no one to go home to anyway." Ouch! I know the comment was not meant to wound. After all, she had not so long before lost her sister, who had lived with her, and her son just two months apart. She was just saying what was true for her as well as for me.

The feeling that came over me during that drive is exactly the same feeling I had experienced dozens of times as I drove home alone from some event or outing, particularly late at night. 'There will be no one to greet me when I arrive home. It's late at night and not one person on this entire Earth knows where I am, what I'm doing, or cares.' The aloneness made me feel like a small, isolated being in a large empty space. I always felt more at ease when I finally walked into my house after lonely drives like these because I felt safe there and knew I was expected to be there by family and friends.

Whether it's a day I take a solitary walk, fix a broken faucet or paint a picture, the ordinary days are what began to define me as separate. Separate from a together life. While I was being redefined on all these ordinary days strung like rosary beads, one after another, it was also where most of my memories lived, and a day never passed without thoughts of Dave—moments spent together, moments becoming new, and even from time to time, moments thinking of the hereafter.

In the Ordinary

Breathing in orange poppy fields
(his favorite flower) as far as
my eye can see wrapping the hillside
as a gift to his memory.

Face turned to the sun ear cocked
my eyes greet the falcon hovering
over the valley suspended by the wind
as if in tribute (to his backyard chair).

Sail north as north can be, the lapis
blue sea (the color of his eyes)
holds fast my heart and our wedding day
and that I love you glance.

The spinning wheels whir in unison
as the peloton of smiling faces
gathers speed up the mountain
(his favorite weekend ride) and there he is.

In the sights I see, places we walked,
laughs we shared, music we loved,
red cars, spinning wheels, and sailing boats,
in the ordinary he is there.

Chapter X
Christmas
Attitude, Adaptation, Transformation

Merely existing was all I could manage for more than a couple of years. There must have been a moment of clarity when I realized I was no better off emotionally. I was drifting and had no clear path. After leaving my job some three years before full retirement age, I found the need to become involved with some other purpose and the challenge to not merely 'be' became paramount. Until that time came around, numbness was my way of life. Eventually, numbness was no longer an option and involvement became an obsession and would later become the foundation for a fuller life with meaning.

When Mike and Matt were young boys, Dave used to make model airplanes with them. After tackling the kind of model airplanes that came in a kit (why would you want something so easy?), Dave decided to make glider airplanes from balsa wood and a special kind of paper (don't ask me what it was). Each glider had a longer wingspan than the next and the last glider he built had a wingspan of seven feet. It was a very serious glider; or I should say, he was very serious about it. Each time one of the gliders was finished, the family would drive to a mountain, sometimes Mt. Diablo, and find a high point with lots of space for gliding. Dave and the boys would launch the planes and they would glide gracefully through the air and, many times, even land gently.

One of the things we discovered after launching a few of these planes was how to launch a glider when it was breezy so that it would reach its targeted destination. Sometimes an aircraft can be blown off-track by winds; by launching the plane to fly in a straight line, the winds can blow the plane off-track and it will land farther south or north of its planned destination. By aiming higher against the direction of the wind, the plane will reach its target destination. Sometimes I felt a little like one of Dave's gliders.

If I did nothing to adjust for the winds and turbulence in life, my destiny might become much less than it was worth. By extending myself and becoming idealistic toward a goal, I reasoned, perhaps I would find meaning and purpose in life. I needed to find that—purpose and meaning. So off I went on a journey of discovery and over-extending.

I joined a non-profit organization, Soroptimist International of America, whose worldwide mission is to improve the lives of women and girls. I was elected to sit as a member on the board of directors for an organization assisting the developmentally disabled. I rejoined my church choir, continued to take piano lessons and attended art workshops. As my friend, Sue, recently pointed out to me, "You were saying 'yes' to absolutely everything." It was true. I was in overdrive, and while this was not necessarily a bad thing, it was a condition that couldn't and wouldn't be sustainable forever. I was, however, determined to find my target destination while being buffeted about by life's turbulence. Defining that target would have been a great idea too. With all the activities that then surrounded me, there was a constant need to keep reminding myself I was looking for meaning and consolation in solitude. Life without Dave.

While I was busy staying busy, life's small, yet challenging moments still crept into the cracks of my hard shell and adjustments to life continued. Winds and turbulence? Minor breezes?

One of these simple, everyday moments oc-curred on December 2, 2011. I was on my way to the grocery store—yep, the grocery store again—to buy small Christmas plants, the kind that come in six-inch pots, stopping at the deli to pick up a sand-wich and soda before heading out on my annual Christmas trek to the cemetery. A small red poin-settia plant and five miniature Christmas trees dec-orated with small silver bells, tiny round ornaments and clear wrapped candies sat in the passenger seat next to me. The trees were for my angels—Dave, Michele, my parents and Dave's mother, Grams (who passed five years after Dave). The poinsettia plant was for Michele. Her birthday would have been six days later and she would have been forty-one, which was totally unthinkable. I still miss her terribly and it seems, as the years roll by, that the aching in my heart doesn't leave me. In some aspect, it still strongly continues to tug at me while I try to find some kind of peace with her loss.

It was a warm day. Even in northern California, a day with temperatures reaching seventy-nine degrees in the month of December is very unusual. I drove to Queen of Heaven Cemetery and parked my car at the end of a row and gathered up my gifts. I offered each little tree to my angels and the plant to Michele and then I settled on a bench next to Dave and Michele to eat my lunch and chat with them. The sun settled on my back and warmed me through as I nibbled on my sandwich. Sometimes I get my biggest ideas and breakthroughs by sitting on this black marble bench, which was installed and dedicated to a young boy and family friend who had passed as a teenager. I frequently find comfort here when I need space to breathe or to clear my head.

Today my angels told me, as they have before, that I had to readjust my thinking. The topic today was all about the holidays. No matter how hard I tried to embrace and hold the traditions of Thanksgiving and Christmas that I had grown up with, and those Dave and I started as we raised our family, there seemed nothing I could do to stop the changes that simply came with time as my children grew older and started their own families and traditions. I'm sure part of this struggle is similar to what other parents experience as their children grow up and the parents find themselves in the 'letting go' syndrome. Letting go seemed doubly hard for me since I had no one with whom I could share and adjust to life's never-ending movement.

I needed to have a talk with myself and take stock of what I could let go of without too much pain and what I needed to try to hold on to tightly as each small holiday tradition and image slipped through my fingers like a sieve. Some were small and inconsequential and easily rolled off me as they fell into an ever-mounting pile of imaginary snowflakes that seemed to surround me, at times holding my feet stationary and fixed.

The latest adjustment came when I tried to arrange a date with Matt to buy my Christmas tree, which had become a tradition of sorts every Christmas since Dave's passing. But this year our calendars were impossible to sync. Every time we tried to find a date that might work, it fell through. I bit the bullet and went out one morning and bought the tree by myself. It wasn't that I couldn't manage toting a small tree or picking out a tree on my own. It was all about doing it alone, without family. One more tradition slipping away?

I was determined to make the best of this situation and I found having the tree lot attendant put my small tree into the back seat of my car felt acceptable and I drove home smelling the scents of pine and Christmas that filled the car. Once home, I pulled my little tree from the car and headed into the family room where I had cleared an end table and covered it with plastic and white snow in preparation for the tree.

Behind the small end table that now held my tiny tree sat two boxes of records. These were LPs that Dave and I had collected before we were married. A few years before his passing, Dave bought a new turntable so we could listen to our old music. It was his 'baby' and I never touched it. He was particular about lifting the arm of the player and gently lowering the diamond needle and gingerly placing it in just the right groove on the record. It had not been used for six years and I had no idea how it worked.

'Can't be that hard,' I told myself. I found two albums of Christmas music. One was Elvis Presley's album *White Christmas* (old and definitely one of mine), and another with Christmas guitar music. I slipped the vinyl from its protective sleeve, tipped the cover of the turntable and found the power On/Off button. As I lowered the diamond needle onto the record, golden tones streamed from the speakers set up around the family room as I gazed at the little Christmas tree waiting to be decorated.

I opened the boxes of ornaments that had been waiting in a closet for a year to be taken out and allowed to shine once again. I strung each branch of my small tree with tiny white lights and small balls. There wasn't a dark or gloomy space anywhere. It was a happy little tree.

At times like that it seemed so simple to move ahead, as if Dave realized my discontent about having to buy, for the first time, a Christmas tree without family.

That day would prove to be more than an afternoon spent with a tree and music. In the evening, as I sat gazing at the tiny tree lights that shown brightly as the sky turned to shades of darkness, I realized the turntable and records gave me a glimpse into how Dave lived life. He addressed life with a code—respect others and be true to yourself. He had a passion about his hobbies and what he chose to do with each day.

These were also the same traits that could drive me crazy. But as I thought about his records and the turntable, I realized something else. He did what he wanted to do without concern for what others thought. He enjoyed life with passion and was true to himself. In the simple act of buying and decorating a tree by myself while listening to music, I learned a lesson that day about living with confidence and holding onto a passion to live life on my own.

It had taken years of actively searching for who I was to be able to receive the gift I learned that day, but it was a turning point. There were and are still days of breakthroughs, and my life was still a seesaw proven not more than two weeks later when Christmas arrived.

Journal Entry:
December 25, 2011

The Christmas Rose blooms during the winter months stretching toward the sun revealing its five snow-white petals. Blooming in the frosty winter snow, it shares only its beauty because it has no thorns, perhaps a reminder that this season is one of joy. Nature is not without its struggles and even this thornless little flower has its struggle for survival. The little plant must push through the bitter cold snow to feel the warmth of the sun.

Preparing for Christmas this year has been a bit like this little flower's struggle to reach the warmth of sunlight, and Christmas Eve proved to be that struggle.

Last night was Christmas Eve 2011 and without a doubt the loneliest one I've ever had. I'm sitting here trying to understand exactly how I am feeling and the only thing I can think of is that I feel hollow. Hollow as if my insides have been carved out leaving an empty shell. It's the kind of pain that isn't in my head. I actually feel the sensation of emptiness in my chest. I can't remember a Christmas Eve when I felt so lonely. Since childhood, it's always been a day filled with family and it has shaken me to realize that there's no one to spend this night with. Mike, Kristen and Max are doing their own Christmas Eve celebrating. I don't know what Matt is doing but, most likely, he went out with friends. I did sing with the choir at the evening services at church. As I sat there listening to the readings and singing with the choir I thought, ' If it weren't for my fellow choir members and being in this church decorated with tall trees for Christmas, my evening would have been totally bleak and empty.' Upon her arrival at the church, a fellow choir member and friend, Ginnie, gave me a big hug, handed me a small gift wrapped in Christmas paper and said, "Merry Christmas!"

When I got home that night I poured myself a glass of wine, sat in front of my little tree with its sparkling lights and tiny glass ornaments and opened the gift from Ginnie and two other small gifts I had received from friends. Opening gifts by myself seemed to shout a-l-o-n-e! Ginnie's gift was very sweet and also thoughtful, an ornament in the shape of a treble clef, the perfect little gift that spoke to our friendship in music. It was perfect, just as perfect as a white-petaled thornless Christmas Rose.

Today is Christmas Day and it will be different. I'll be with the family, exchange gifts and have a wonderful meal.

And so it was.

Transformation

Rising morning
Lays down to nightfall,
Was there more

Atrophy of life
Suspended dreams
Ticking clock

The core wells
With restless spirit
Hopes and clarity

Restful slumber
Awake the morning
Bounteous life

Chapter XI
The Excuse

After a couple of years I was able to emotionally settle back into a life routine, and even though I was still caring for my mother-in-law, my job became even busier as my boss and I started a tour of three of the five states where our company had offices. This meant trips to different parts of California, Washington and Hawaii. I was particularly excited about going to Hawaii since I have family roots there. The last time I visited the islands was with Dave and Matt several years before and I was ready to return.

As anyone who travels on business will tell you, it's not as glamorous and not nearly as much fun as it sounds. Once we reached Honolulu, we had a crazy schedule that took us to four of the islands in three days. Each morning started by visiting our local office to give a presentation, then off to the airport to fly to a neighboring island to prepare for another office presentation. One day we flew twice in order to visit all the offices within the allotted time frame and we were in paradise, but exhausted.

Is there a beach in Hawaii? If so, I barely saw it and certainly didn't venture to the water's edge until we reached the island of Kauai. I vowed to myself that on this island, where I always feel rooted and connected to family, I would hit the beach for some quiet time. My father, his three brothers and sister were born and raised on this island, as were my grandparents.

We checked into our accommodations late in the evening and I set my alarm clock for 5:00 a.m.

I barely slept as I waited for the alarm clock to go off and when it did, I sprang to my feet and brewed coffee, pouring it into a big mug I grabbed on my way out the door. I stepped out onto the white sand and planted myself on the beach to watch the orange-red glow of the rising sun as it cast sparkles across the crystal-clear water. Waves raced to the shore and washed back over black lava leaving bubbles of foam in its wake—water as far as my eye could see. The horizon stretched to meet some airy clouds forming in the distance. I breathed in every inch of the scene and felt a gentle breeze as it rustled the fringe-shaped fronds of a palm tree that hung its arched arms gracefully towards the water. Heaven on Earth. If only I could stay forever.

I soaked in the scene to recall another time because I knew this kind of peace was only in this moment. Reflections took me to another time when I met Dave here while he was on R&R from his time served in Vietnam, but in this beautiful place it wasn't necessary to steal myself from his absence. I felt at peace here. My time on Kauai's lovely and isolated beach was all too short. I did have a meeting to attend. I kicked the sand from my flip-flops as I made my way back to my room, unaware that the travel bug was about to take hold.

Dave and I had been to Europe a few times, but travel was far and few between for us because, while we were raising our family, we never seemed to have enough extra money to splurge on vacations for ourselves. I certainly had never traveled alone. In contrast, my friend Linda had traveled extensively, with her husband, co-workers and friends.

Sometimes the synchronicity of life is more than I could ever dream or imagine. Linda and I met in the early years of our marriages while I worked and waited for Dave's return from Vietnam; while she and her husband at the time started to raise a family. As in the case of the bewildering coincidence with my cousin, Arlene, whose husband passed too young, Linda's husband passed some five months after Dave. It is truly uncanny. But she let me know if I ever decided to take a trip, she'd be ready to join me.

It was at one of those moments when I felt so lonely I wanted to scream that I looked at a travel catalogue I had signed up to receive from a tour company Linda had used several times. I paged through the dream book and found a tour to Norway that sounded wonderful.

My heritage is half Norwegian and I had missed an opportunity to travel there years before when my mother, her sister and a cousin all went to Norway and had asked me to go along. Family responsibilities and money stopped me from joining them. This time, I don't know why I didn't call

Linda to ask her if she wanted to go with me, but for some reason I just picked up the phone, called the tour company and put down my deposit.

I emailed Linda to tell her the news. "Now what do I think I'm doing? I just booked a trip to Norway," I wrote. Shortly after I sent the email, my phone rang. It was Linda.

"You can't go without me. If you wait until May, I can go with you," she said. I sighed a bit of relief since I had to admit to myself that I was just a little apprehensive about going on a two-week trip overseas by myself. But now I was excited and reasoned that since we would be going in May it would be a perfect birthday gift to myself. I would justify this trip any way I could.

I was looking forward to visiting Bergen and Trondheim where my grandparents had been born and raised and to see the country of my ancestors. Waiting the several months until the day I would step on a plane and venture out to a new country and new experiences kept my mind occupied, and the travel books I read flooded me with anticipation. It seemed the perfect antidote for my loneliness.

Although I had thought about the fact that May is my birthday month, one day while sitting on the small cruise ship that sailed us up the entire coast of Norway, I sat writing in my journal in front of a large observation window and realized it was the anniversary date of Dave's passing. A melancholy settled over me and I took another deep breath as I watched the beautiful fjords outside the window. My journal entry that day was short:

> Journal Entry:
> May 22, 2007
> (two-year anniversary)
>
> Dear One:
> Just sailed over the Arctic Circle— still wish you were here. Arctic Circle marked by a globe of the world on a small island (rock really) port side of the ship. Water—lapis blue ... Would love to share this with you.

Of course, sharing this with him wasn't going to happen and I accepted the partial comfort of the moment by drinking in the scenery. I was moving past my front door and trying to move my life along the best I could. I had a lot to learn about accepting reality, but at that moment I thought I was, at the very least, making small strides.

My twenty-one tour mates proved to be wonderful traveling companions and while most were couples, there were a few other single people besides Linda and me. About eight of our group became close-knit and founded what we would loosely call The Aquavit Club. Early one freezing morning our ship berthed for a few hours in the town of Hammerfest. The town claims to be the northernmost city in the world and our little group was determined to get off the ship and have a small toast to this quiet northern city. At 5:30 a.m. in the freezing cold, we stole down the gangplank as quietly as possible, and, with only a couple of hours until the ship would sail again, made our way to the town hall looking for an appropriate place to make our toast.

At this early hour we found the town almost empty. One of our group, Bill, had stashed a small bottle of Aquavit under his jacket while the rest of us clutched little glasses or paper cups in our pockets that we'd use for a small shot of the elixir. On a hillside was a small gazebo that bore the town's latitude and longitude and seemed to be the perfect spot. In large white numbers across the pale blue structure it read: latitude +70.68 (70°40'48"N) longitude +23.71 (23°42'36"E) in validation of the status the town claimed.

We had our tiny drinks, which weren't even enough to warm us as we huddled together under our layers of jackets and scarves, toasting our ship and its travelers and wishing safe passage during the remainder of our trip. We moved through the little town to the only building left standing after WWII, the Hauen Church, where we watched a reindeer with short, fuzzy antlers munching grass, the only other living creature to brave the cold. He didn't seem to notice our presence; and if he did, he didn't care. I have since learned that during early spring each year, Hammerfest is a migration path to some 3,000 reindeer annually. I can't image the residents are pleased with Santa's pals taking over the town each spring.

It was moments like this, while trying to reach out past my little world to a much larger world, that gave me moments of clarity. There were people to meet, things to learn, experiences to relish and life to live.

Over the years, that first trip, like water cascading down a mountainside, led to other trips and I made other traveling memories in Italy, France, Croatia, Slovenia and Ireland.

Italy. Oh, how I love Venice! One year I met my son, Mike, daughter-in-law, Kristen and grandson, Max, at the train station on the island of Venice to begin a seven-day stay with them. As I stood on the station's steps that led to the Grand Canal, I watched each *vaporetto* as it pulled up to the dock, waiting for my family to disembark. Finally a boat pulled up and out popped Max. I saw him looking around trying to find me. I was so excited I started waving my arms in the air so he would see me. His eyes caught sight of me and he came running full steam ahead—sandy blond hair flopping with arms outstretched as he crashed into my arms.

My grandmother's heart was melting and a few tear droplets sprinkled my cheek. Max looked up and said, "Grama, why are you crying?"

"I'm just so happy to see you, Max."

That's all I could say because it was the simple truth. I'll always have this sweet image of my five-year-old grandson as one of 'those' memories to cherish and hold onto.

We took the train from Venice to Florence and arrived at the flat where I would spend a week with my family. We toured, we ate—gelato, lots of gelato—drank our fill of Italian wine and never got our fill of hot croissants, prosciutto and cheese. At the end of the week it was hard to say good-bye to my family. They would stay in their Italian flat on a little side street in Florence for another two weeks, but I was on my way home.

France—what isn't there to love about France? Once again I traveled with my friend, Linda. We arrived at our Paris hotel, which was strategically located just two short blocks from the Champs Elysees and the Arc de Triomphe. I'll never forget strolling that broad avenue at midnight, soaking in all the sights and sounds of a stream of buzzing people chatting, eating and laughing into the wee hours of the night. Directly across the street from our hotel was a small café with people flowing out onto the sidewalk and sitting at tables for two.

It was like a small magnet that pulled us in one afternoon as we sat in the warm Paris sun munching on baguettes and cheese.

"This is like something out of a movie," we said to each other through muffled giggles. The waiter came toward us and asked, partly in French and partly in English, what wine we would like. We had no idea, so he said, "I'll just bring the jug."

"What's the jug?" we whispered to each other—more muffled giggles. The jug wine was fine and the waiter never did explain the jug to us, but we later decided it was just what you might consider their house wine. It was France—how bad could the house wine be?

Monet's garden in Giverny was another amazing site and I strolled the gardens, walked around his Japanese-inspired pond snapping pictures of each bloom in the garden, the Japanese bridge and the rooms in his cottage-style house. The kitchen was painted a cornflower blue, and what wasn't painted was tiled in blue ceramic; and the dining room was a brilliant yellow that defied words. It screamed of sunshine and joy.

Each journey to these foreign countries had their own stories, and each journey brought new acquaintances, new adventures and a breadth of knowledge and distraction. But without exception there came a moment on each of these trips when it became painfully obvious that for all the experiences I was enjoying, I still felt Dave's absence. Shouldn't he be strolling the Champs Elysees with me, sipping that glass of jug wine in that small café, roaming the gardens of Monet?

I wrestled with my motivations for all this travel. Yes, I was meeting people and learning; but, was I also running? Running away from facing facts. Or was I rushing toward making a new life? A finely-drawn line separated those two monumental images and it had me trekking around the globe searching for more away time.

When each trip ended, my return brought me right back to my front door. I would open it and my life was right where I had left it with all my memories, choices and lists. In many ways, it was comforting to find everything exactly as I left it. It was also sobering when I realized I was still missing Dave, and by taking baby steps it would take a long time to readjust my life. I had to wonder: Why all this traveling?

There would be one trip in my future, however, that would give purpose to my traveling baby steps and leave no doubt I was not just running away.

Should I Look For You?

Could I find you
in the blue lapis waters of the Arctic Circle
or the steep crags of the fjords of Norway?

Were you there somewhere
in that little café in Paris
drinking the jug wine and watching over me?

Should I have looked for you
walking through Monet's garden
or in the soupy canals of Venice?

Was I too far away
but not close enough to hear your voice
in the hushed caves of Lascaux?

In all the traveling
did I miss the truth that you have been
here in my heart all the time?

Chapter XII
The Trip

I was at a Soroptimist club meeting when I first met Mary Tuchscherer. She is the founder of a non-profit, VoiceFlame Writers International (now called VoiceFlame), whose goal is to give voice to the women of Malawi, Africa through learning a writing practice called the Amherst Writers and Artists (AWA) method. She was at our club meeting in January 2010 to give a slide presentation, to share pictures and the story of her organization's last trip to Malawi and to explain the goals of her organization. I watched the slide presentation as she pitched our club for a donation that would provide a writing scholarship for one woman in Malawi to be awarded during the organization's next trip.

I was intrigued by her presentation for two reasons. One reason was the feeling that takes hold of many of us when we see photos of the underprivileged, especially women and children in developing countries. I thought how wonderful it would be to actually go to this small African country to meet these women with the hope of helping them live better and fuller lives. Mary talked about Voice-Flame and how, through teaching these women the AWA method of writing, they would be able to find their own voices to tell the stories of their lives. Wow, all I could think of was how incredible this could be. The second reason (perhaps on a more selfish level), was that I wondered if this method of writing would help me in the pursuit of writing my own story. As during other times of my grieving process, I felt I had hit a definite and, in some respects, finite roadblock with my writing.

For as far back as I can remember, or at least since I learned to read, one of my passions has been poetry: reading it and writing it. I grew up with two artistic parents who both painted and wrote poetry. My bookcases hold many works of poetry, most gifted to me over the years by Dave, family and friends. When I need to pour my soul into something tangible, it is always in writing. Whether it takes the form of journal writing or prose, I must write. Writing never ceased for me, even when I had days when I could not think about writing this book.

After the meeting that day, I sat with Mary for a few minutes and we talked about the book I hoped to complete and how her work with the women of Malawi had grabbed my heart. While discussing the AWA method of writing, I learned it is a well-known program for writers in the U.S. and several other countries, and that a woman, Pat Schneider, who now lives in Amherst, Massachusetts, founded it in the 1980s. I was enthralled.

The moment's enthusiasm evaporated as month after month rolled into a year since Mary and I had chatted about her work and writing. Then, during one of my monthly Soroptimist board meetings, Mary's name came up again. One of our board members was reading an email she had received from Mary. VoiceFlame was preparing to embark on its next trip to Malawi and there were still two spots available for women who were interested in going. "Please ask the Soroptimist club members if anyone would like to find out more about the trip," the email requested.

The synchronicity of life overwhelmed me again. I had been struggling with writing and sometimes weeks would roll by, perhaps even a month, when it was proving to be impossible. I had ignored the knock at my door a year before when I talked with Mary the first time and now I heard a second knock. My first question, to myself, which would turn out to be one of many, was 'Do I turn my back on this opportunity again?' I felt as if someone was hitting me on the side of my head, saying, "Hello, wake up!"

The next day I called Mary and reintroduced myself and asked about the trip. She suggested we meet for coffee to discuss it. At eight o'clock the next morning, I found myself sitting at Starbucks in Lafayette chatting and laughing with Mary as if we were old friends. We sat there for over an hour and from time to time I had the sense our conversation was actually a kind of interview. In retrospect, I can certainly understand why. The trip was not for the faint of heart and this trip was not a vacation with five-star hotels and fine dining. There would be no Aquavit Club. There would, however, be eight women on this trip living in very close quarters and the last thing the group needed was someone who didn't share some of the 'heart' needed to reach out to other women in a country of poverty, disease, abuse and orphaned children. A binding commonality was needed in order for the trip to be cohesive and, most importantly, to attain the goals of touching the lives of the women and girls in Malawi.

During our conversation I finally got around to some basics. Malawi is, after all, a developing country and one of the nine poorest countries in the world with one of the highest levels of HIV/AIDS.

"Is the trip safe?" I asked.

"Oh, yes," Mary assured me.

"What about snakes," I asked.

"Well, we didn't see any the last time we were there," Mary said. '*Oh*,' I thought, '*that's reassuring.*' I asked about the food, bathroom facilities, vaccinations and other equally menial questions, thinking somehow the answers would help me make a decision about whether or not to go on this trip.

"I can picture you sitting in a circle with us in the evening sharing each day's adventure," she said.

I guessed I had passed the test, whatever that might have been, and I sensed I was being asked to come along. I wasn't sure if I wanted to go. I needed time to think about all the potential 'adventures' this trip might hold. I had three days to make my decision and all I could hear was Mary saying, not once, but several times, "We have to be open to miracles, adventures and the unexpected."

It seemed those were the only guarantees. She pointed to the wall behind me that provided a resting place for my back. I turned, looked up and there were several paintings of African natives on the wall. I smiled. Coincidence?

I spent two sleepless nights trying to process the pros and cons of this trip until I realized there was no way on Earth I could predict what could happen in a third-world country I'd never visited, or any third-world country for that matter. I had no point of reference, no experience with the poverty, orphaned children or abused women I might meet. I was also worried, to the point of obsession, about the wildlife, mostly the snakes, which crept into my mind more than any reasonable person might obsess. Hippos and snakes, oh my! Not to make light of the wildlife—hippos can be extremely dangerous and aggressive and Africa does have some of the most poisonous snakes on the planet.

While I was trying to make a decision about accepting the invitation to go on this trip I was conversing with an acquaintance who happened to be a psychologist. She listened patiently to my tirade about hippos and then casually commented, "It's called disproportionate response syndrome." Okay, great. That made me feel 'normal!' I now knew the name of the syndrome that I realized my sons kept telling me I had. The cost of the trip also raised a red flag, but I reasoned it was no more expensive than the vacations and touristy trips I had taken over the prior five years.

I came to one decision almost immediately. I would not ask Mike, Matt or any of my friends for their input. This had to be my decision alone. My friends would tell me I shouldn't go for medical reasons, or my safety, or they would just say I was crazy and shouldn't go. I wasn't sure what my sons would think. No, this had to be my decision alone. There was that word again—alone. But, it was true.

I searched the Internet for all things Malawi, reading blogs from others who had been there. Mary sent me a tentative schedule of the villages and towns we would most likely visit. I researched those villages and checked out what little there was from a tourist's point of view, although I knew this was not a tourist destination. After spending hours searching, I was still nowhere near ready to make a decision. In this, the Internet was not helpful.

This decision had to be based on more than just the country or the wildlife that inhabited its countryside. It was a decision of the heart. Did I want to help make a difference in the lives of women who had much less than I could even imagine? Did I want to delve more deeply into who I was becoming by writing with the women I would be traveling with, who were also writers? Did I want to share my story through writing with women from a culture literally worlds apart from my own? Was I ready for another journey that only had the guarantees of miracles, adventures and the unexpected?

Three days later I called Mary and said, "Yes." I allowed myself for the first time to get excited about all the possibilities of this journey and I could not wait to tell Mike and Matt. I met Mike for lunch one afternoon, and as we sat on the terrace of a restaurant that sits on the Oakland Estuary watching sailboats glide by, I built up my courage before pulling out a map of Malawi from my purse. I placed the map on the table in front of him—like this was going to totally explain everything and he would automatically buy into the trip on which I was about to embark. I explained the mission and goals of Voice-Flame and waited for Mike's response.

"It gets hot in Africa, Mom. Are you sure this will be okay with your MS?" I had my answer ready because one of the women I would be traveling with had a son who just happened to be a doctor working in Malawi, and my neurologist had given me medication to take if I should experience an MS episode. I felt prepared, at least as prepared as a person can be as she ventures out into the unknown.

With map and story, I reenacted the same account of my plans while having dinner with Matt. He said, "It gets hot in Africa, Mom. Are you sure this will be okay with your MS?"

I love that I have two sons who really do care about my health. They get a bit frustrated with me, I think, from time to time, because it appears I'm not paying attention to the potential problems my health could cause if I'm not careful. I do recognize my limitations though, and I must say they are small in the scheme of life, and I was learning I couldn't sit and watch life run over me.

So, off I went to travel some 10,300 miles away, as the crow flies, for three weeks. If I had been running it would have been the farthest I had traveled to get away, but this time running wasn't part of the plan.

Facing The Real

As if another place could change the real,
Leaving home remedy the now,
Or busy work replace the always.

Worlds cannot blank the then and now
            memory of sight
                        touch
                            love
      and certainly not always.

No choice but to carry him with me
      facing the real, the real of loss
                            miss
                                love
            then now and always.

Chapter XIII
The Other Side of the World

After four months of planning, conference calls with my seven travelling companions, reading everything I could get my hands on about Malawi and receiving the appropriate immunizations, I thought I was prepared to trek to a developing country.

Journal Entry:
May 3, 2011

I awoke at 5:30 a.m., showered, dressed and wandered the house making sure all was in order. And then, I got nervous. I tried quiet reflection, eyes closed, sitting comfortably, white light in, darkness out. Breathing shallow. It wasn't helping. I did my favorite qigong moves and . . . and, I realized I was so tense I had a pencil point sharp pain under my right back wing. So . . . I went to the piano and played until the doorbell rang. That worked. Mary had arrived and we were on our way to the San Francisco airport . . .

As our plane touched down in New York City, I turned on my cell phone to retrieve voice mail messages. "You have one voice mail message." I hit PLAY MESSAGE and listened to the South Africa Airline representative tell me that my flight to Johannesburg, scheduled for the next day, had been cancelled. 'This is not a good sign,' I told myself. But, I was in the same boat with three of my traveling companions, Mary, Susan and Julie, and we all still had our feet planted on U.S. terra firma, so how bad could this really be?

We were in New York City, and that is not the worst place in the world to spend an extra day and perhaps eat some great food. Julie had a niece and nephew living nearby so she called them, and they agreed to meet us for dinner at a rib joint called Blue Smoke that described their cuisine as 'urban barbecue.' They were very interested in hearing about our trip and the work VoiceFlame hoped to accomplish during our time working with women and girls in Malawi. As we all finished eating, there wasn't one of us who wasn't licking barbecue sauce off our fingers—it was really good stuff. We were having a wonderful time sitting around chatting about the trip until we realized we had a fifteen-hour flight coming up with the sun, and it definitely called for a good night's sleep. With big hugs and well wishes for a wonderful trip we parted company and with rain gently falling in New York City we headed back to our accommodations for the night.

Adjustments were made and the day finally arrived, May 6, 2011, when I found myself sitting on a plane with four of my traveling companions headed toward the southeastern part of Africa and the small land-locked country of Malawi. There was no turning back.

During the fifteen-hour, almost sleepless flight from New York to Johannesburg, I thought I would have plenty of time to wonder and dream about the adventure I was about to embark upon. Instead, I sat like an unwilling captive next to a man from Swaziland. He was returning home from his first visit to the U.S. and was thrilled he had been able to see the White House during his three-day trip to Washington, D.C. After a few hours of easy conversation he began to relax and that's when I knew it was going to be a very long fifteen hours.

I look back on his habits now and wonder if a lot of his actions were simply cultural. We did come from two very different cultures. It's hard for a westerner to understand how throwing food wrappers and uneaten food on the floor is okay; how resting the open book that you're reading on your neighbor's arm, since your space is full of stuff, is okay; or how taking my earphone headset to try on is okay, just because he wonders if the sound is the same as it is through his headset; and most of all, how it's okay to sleep on your neighbor's headrest! We, of course, have a phrase for this—invading one's personal space. By the end of the flight, my feet had trash piled up around them and I had no place to put my head. It was not a pleasant flight, although I was glad my neighbor was excited about his visit to the U.S. and the White House. I realized I had a lot to learn about people from other lands.

After a short layover in Johannesburg and another two-and-a-half hour flight, we finally arrived at our destination: Lilongwe, Malawi, Africa.

A Malawian woman, Emily, who would be our leader and guide for our three-week visit, met us at the Lilongwe Airport. My journal speaks to my first impression upon arriving in this country.

> Journal Entry:
> sometime between
> May 6 and May 7, 2011
>
> After twenty-two hours of flying time I am totally in the dark about what day it is. I tell myself that, frankly, it doesn't really matter.
> My first impression of this country, when I got off the plane, was that I had just arrived in Hawaii. There was Red Ginger blooming, Silk Trees with bright orange blossoms and huge green plants that looked like Taro. We loaded into our little caravan bus that would be our cocoon for the next several weeks with seats enough to accommodate the eight of us, Emily, Roderick, our driver, and our luggage piled in a heap at the back. We were all excitement and smiles.

But this was only the dressing, and in no way reflected the heart of the adventure that was about to begin.

There are many individual stories I could share about the daily adventures, miracles and the unexpected while on this trip as well as the vulnerable moments, but perhaps that will be another book. Two days after my return from this trip and with an overwhelmed spirit that could not be contained, I shared the following in the form of an email with my friends and family.

> . . . after twenty-four hours of flying time, which included four separate flights and being awake for over forty hours, I finally arrived home. My three-week trip is impossible to summarize in a few sentences or even a few paragraphs. Meeting the villagers of Chewa, Tonga and Ngoni tribes was overwhelming. They showed great joy and hope in the midst of tremendous poverty and disease.

Ink flowed from my pen like a broken water tap. The miracles, adventures and the unexpected were now revealed and they screamed of a culture that taught me about the disparity of life and the needs of a people from a land so far away, yet now so close.

I owe the opportunity for this once-in-a-lifetime experience to Mary and her organization, VoiceFlame. While we were there to assist women find their voices through writing, I found I was discovering and learning as well—learning about their culture, their lives, and their many needs. I was living an experience that would also teach me a bit about myself. We traveled to the mountaintop village of Livingstonia, named after David Livingston by one of his followers in the early 1900s. Our lodging was in a building built by the village founders and we shared our accommodations with the local bats.

The morning after we arrived, we walked to Livingstonia University where we met with some thirty women students and teachers. We broke into groups of six or eight and two of us from Voice-Flame led each group. Julie and I were paired together as leaders that morning with a group of six Malawian women. Our writing assignment was to reflect on several colorful fabrics that had been piled in the middle of the room on the floor for all to see. What story would come to each of us in our little group? I wondered. What would we share? How would this help these women share, through the written word, their stories of living in a repressed culture with so many needs?

I stared at the pile of cloth. It was not speaking to me! My mind went blank until I reached far back in my memory to remember my mom teaching me how to sew. I wrote about . . . *a day when Mom came into my room and said we were going shopping. We jumped in her car, we bought fabric and she taught me to sew.* While writing, I thought it was a pretty ordinary story, but at least I had something down on paper to share.

One of the fabrics that covered the floor was a deep red cloth with designs of war shields, clay pots and pairs of crossed spears. One of the Malawian women in our group had chosen this fabric as her subject. She was a member of the Ngoni tribe and this particular piece of fabric happened to be her tribe's design. While listening to her read her story, inspired by her tribe's cloth, I learned that a clay pot is given to each newly married couple. It is a symbol of womanhood. The woman will carry this pot on her head representing the balance her husband expects her to maintain in their marriage. If the woman should break the pot, she will try to find money from somewhere to replace it before her husband finds out. If she can't, he may beat her as the accepted punishment for breaking the valuable vessel. As the woman continued to read her story and explain the meaning of the pot, she ended by saying, "The pot is a symbol of myself and I am empty from all my work."

Then it was my turn to read my story to the women. When I finished they all made comments about how blessed and lucky I was to have a mother who loved me so much. That is when I realized how my casual recitation of an ordinary day in my life would be an extraordinary day in their lives—my own room, a car, a store, buying cloth and a mother who taught me how to sew. All the things of an ordinary American girl's life, but not a life that any of these women would ever have or could even relate to. I felt a little embarrassed. I have so much I take for granted. They have so little. But it was also the perfect sharing of our cultures.

The week before, we had been welcomed at Tukombo Girls High School in a large auditorium by some four hundred cheering young high school girls. Originally it had been arranged for us to write with only the seniors, about one hundred students, and we were prepared. When we saw the room packed with the entire student body we were struck as if by lightning. The headmaster casually commented that he had made the decision to include all the students because he didn't want any of them to miss out on the opportunity to write with us. After the initial shock, we gathered in a huddle and put our heads together to figure out how to write with so many students.

The girls were eager and perhaps even a bit restless not knowing what to expect. After telling them the process for writing, they would be given a topic to guide their thoughts as they wrote and then a few of the students would volunteer to share their stories, we began. We taught them the signal to use when they had finished—clap your hands, stomp your feet in a rhythmic pattern. There are no cultural barriers for some things and clapping and stomping seemed to be a universal high school ritual. They loved it. Those that shared the stories they had written talked of their dreams and they dreamed big. It was an amazing afternoon and, as we left the girls and said our goodbyes later that afternoon, their cheers and enthusiasm floated us toward our little mini-bus. Before leaving, the headmaster told us that he never knew teaching could be so much fun. We were invited back the next night to see the girls in a dramatic play they had been rehearsing for a local competition. They were inspiring young women. We hope they will have better lives than those Malawian women who contract HIV/AIDS and leave orphaned children, from those whose lives have been cut short, from those who are sexually abused and from those who are never asked to share their stories.

During our trip we also visited a feeding center for orphaned children. They touched our hearts deeply and, one of our company, Robbyn, was bound and determined to make a change, however small, by touching these children's lives with something each could call their own. As we sat on the porch of our Livingstonia lodgings one night, watching the moon rise in the steel-blue sky, a new non-profit was born, *Animals For Africa*. Its goal is to form sewing circles in the United States to hand stitch small stuffed animals for each orphan in Malawi.

Each day while in Malawi our lives were impacted by the women we met as we witnessed their joy, their enthusiasm for life and their deep desire to change that which seems to be their fate, one of repression and disease. Once I had met and shared and worked with these women, after I knew them by name—Emily, Mbumba, David, Sarah, Pilirani, Bhatupe, and others—there was no leaving them behind. They remain a vision real and vivid, and the red Malawi dust swirled around my heart like licks of a flame and settled in.

One might imagine this trip, in and of itself, was the only experience that impacted me in Africa. While to an extent this is true, it is only part of the truth. I was traveling with seven wonderful women—Mary, Sue, Julie, Robbyn, Kari, Susan and Jane—and they hailed from different parts of the

U.S. and Canada. The binding tie was that we were all writers, and during our three-week trek, when time allowed and we hadn't succumbed to exhaustion, we would write together sharing our reflections of the day, our trip and our experiences. I learned from each of them, in their own individual ways, lessons in the giving of their talents and of themselves, and I witnessed great empathy for those less fortunate. I learned how to be a better writer by listening to the stories and reflections they had written and shared, and felt the warmth of living among women with a common bond.

Reflections on this trip and the connectedness with others went on for months until I realized I had finally stopped thinking Dave was just around the corner, and that it was all right for me to live my life without him.

I didn't have to go halfway around the world to make this discovery, but one of the differences between this journey and others I had taken over the preceding five years was the lesson I learned about the needs of people; whether they were in another country ten thousand miles away, in my own country or my own community, and how I could be of service to others.

The other difference was timing. Prior to this trip, with all the ups and downs of my emotional life and without being consciously aware of it, I was in a cocoon waiting for the time when I would be ready to escape into a new life that had worth in my unwanted role of being alone. It took time to unravel the emotional trauma of my losses, both my loss of Dave and my loss of Michele. When I embarked on this trip to Malawi, I was ready at that particular point in time to be able to receive the gifts of awareness and the understanding of the life that lay before me, one with purpose.

At the end of that year, I sat before my festive, decorated tree on Christmas Eve 2011 with a glass of wine and a few gifts I had received from friends. After opening the gifts, I sat listening to music as I absentmindedly twisted my engagement ring. I was thinking about being alone on this day that had always been filled with family. The ring slipped off my finger. The size-six ring that Dave had slipped onto my finger some forty-four years ago had just come off my now size-eight finger. I had not been able to get this ring off for over ten years. It was physically impossible, but the impossible happened.

Liwonde Night

The guide cut the engine of the
safari jeep and the sounds
of the Malawi wilderness
crashed upon my ears.

With eyes shut I tried to record
the sounds as to never forget
the symphony that stirred me
into a kind of rapture.

A hundred, no a thousand
clicking crickets, frogs croaking
and buzzing from what creature?
joining the chorus.

Memory is not capable of exact
recollection which makes me sad
for it was all for that moment
that one unforgettable night of music.

For the next night it did not return.

Chapter XIV
Stepping Past the Past

For the following year after returning from Malawi, life became busy helping VoiceFlame in its mission to assist the women and girls in this third world country, then I joined their board of directors. It is a worthwhile organization and I knew, even if I never personally returned to Malawi, I could still make a contribution with my time by becoming involved with this non-profit. My life also became very full with my friends, my art, my music, and I found myself volunteering and becoming involved with other non-profit work as well.

Much of the time I felt I had found a new rhythm in life. There were still ups and downs certainly, but some smooth roads as well as I took some rather big steps into the unknown. There always seemed to be one more challenge to face without Dave. A new challenge started after a wonderful four-day getaway to Virginia where I reunited with five of the women with whom I had traveled to

Malawi. After lazy, sunny days reminiscing about our trip and enjoying each other's company, I returned to a house that had been burglarized.

I had stepped past the threshold of my house and closed the door on my world thinking, as I had in the past, that I would return and find the security of house and home intact and right where I had left it.

Paula had picked me up at the Lafayette BART rail station after my flight home to the San Francisco airport, and as we drove into my driveway she asked if I always kept all my lights on when I go away.

"I don't," I said. We entered the house and I realized that not only were all the lights on, but the window blinds in the kitchen were open. I never leave them open when I'm gone. Someone had been in my home.

As I approached the bottom of the stairs that go up to my bedroom, I could see the dresser drawers lying on the floor. The house had been ransacked. I immediately went to my safe that was tucked away in the guest room closet—gone. Every piece of fine jewelry Dave had given me—gone. My mother's, both grandmothers' and my mother-in-law's jewelry were also taken, as well as every piece of costume jewelry I owned. My passport was taken and, of course, they had walked off with my laptop computer.

I immediately called the police and they arrived in less than ten minutes. The thieves had broken in through a dining room window and waltzed out the back sliding door taking my treasures with them. I felt such a deep sense of violation and of being trespassed upon that a tightening in my stomach was making me feel ill.

There is no replacing all the sentiment, memories or past history linked to each piece of jewelry Dave had gifted to me over the years. No replacing the brooch my grandmother had given me—a brooch she wore on her wedding dress in Norway in the late 1800s, and no replacing Michele's jewelry box that had also been taken.

After the police talked with me, investigated the scene and left, Paula and I walked around looking at the mess left in the wake of the thieves and then we opened a bottle of wine. I was a nervous wreck and exhausted from my flight home and I knew I couldn't stay in the house that night, so I checked into a hotel for the evening. The next day would be soon enough to deal with the aftermath.

The first few nights I spent in the house alone were uncomfortable. For the first time in the thirty-five years my family had lived in this house, I didn't feel safe. Within a few days I called a security alarm company and had a security system installed. I was angry. It was bad enough that these faceless thieves had taken so much from me, both physically and emotionally, but now I felt like a puppet jumping through hoops trying to put things in order and having to spend both emotional and physical energy, not to mention money, to get what could be set right put back together.

Besides having to have a broken window and screen door fixed, there was also a list of things to do. Yes, another list. There were things taken and a list to compile for the police report and insurance company, a call had to be made to the U.S. State Department to cancel my stolen passport and a new passport had to be secured. The expense of a new laptop computer to replace my less than two-year-old computer that contained thousands of cherished photos, an iMovie I created of the trip to Malawi that was being used at events to promote Voice-Flame and the original draft of this manuscript, left me shaking my head in disbelief.

One bright shining moment, which helped me through this ordeal, was the day when my son, Mike, was dropping off my grandson, Max, to spend a week with me. It was less than a week after the day I came home to find my house broken into and I was not in the best emotional state. Max walked into the house and handed me a gift bag. I opened the bag to find a small gift box tied with a white satin ribbon and a card. I opened the card and read the inscription, 'Just because we love you.' Mike, Kristen and Max had all signed their names. As I choked back tears, I opened the small box and pulled out a velvety pouch. I slowly opened the soft pouch and found a silver heart dangling from a beautiful sterling silver bracelet. I couldn't contain the droplets of tears that sprinkled my cheeks.

Once again Max was asking me, "Why are you crying, Grama?" And once again, all I could say was, "Because I'm happy." Someday, I know he'll understand how tears can equal happiness as well as sadness. Then Mike said, "I know this doesn't replace everything you've lost." But on some level it did. The thoughtfulness of this gift overwhelmed me and affirmed what a blessing my children are to me.

After Max's visit, I was again faced with all the insecurities I felt about having been burglarized. I don't really know if these feelings of insecurity and a new wave of loneliness during those first few nights alone in the house somehow figured into the next steps I found myself taking, or if the reunion with my friends had something to do with it. Perhaps it was a little of both. Two of my friends were moving ahead in their lives with boyfriends and were pretty darn happy. I felt encouraged as they talked to me and asked when I was going to make a move in the same direction in finding someone special.

Whatever the reason, within a week after putting my house back in order, I picked up the phone and called a dating service. On-line date searching seemed like it would be so time consuming and the thought of browsing dozens of bios just seemed overwhelming. No, the local dating service would be better. I was given an appointment for a consultation and things would move forward from there.

When the day of the consultation arrived, I walked into a small greeting area in an office in the middle of San Francisco's financial district. The lobby had a very stylish sofa and armchair with leopard print throw pillows. 'Wow,' I thought. 'This is rather, I don't know what—over the top?' Was this supposed to be sexy or just scary enough to make me want to run? If nothing else, it made me ask myself, 'What are you doing here?'

After I chatted with a cute, young receptionist, I was shown into a small office and a petite, well-put-together woman (in her forties, I guessed) chatted with me about their program, the success rate of matching couples and how their service worked. I explained to her that my husband had unexpectedly passed away several years before.

"Why do you think you're ready to date?" she asked, surprising me. I mouthed some words that seem plausible at the moment, but I had to admit to myself that I hadn't really given the answer to that question a great deal of thought. I was just acting and responding to some need to reach out for some companionship. Toward the end of our conversation, she cocked her head and smiled at me and said, "I still see your sadness." That was because I was still sad and I wasn't exactly sure what I was doing.

I thought I'd like to try going out with a few men to see if I even wanted to consider finding someone for companionship. I wanted to be able to go out, have a nice dinner and some conversation and discover where this might take me.

As I prepared to leave and we both moved from our chairs and walked toward her office door she said softly, "You do know you need to take your wedding rings off?" Yes, I knew that, and I explained to her that I hadn't been able to get my wedding band off for many years because it was so small. (Unlike the Christmas Eve when my engagement ring slipped off my finger, my wedding band never budged.)

"I have to have it cut off," I told her.

"I'm sorry," she whispered.

By the end of the interview, I had bitten the bullet and signed up for a conservative four-date agreement. I can do this, I told myself. The service would match me with four men who would meet me for dinners. The agency would arrange every-thing—for a high price, and I was prepared for that, too. I had chosen not to try this online, and dating services do cost more money. It still seemed the more conservative and right route for me.

After the agency meeting, I met Paula for lunch at the Cheesecake Factory that was a few doors away from the dating service's office. She had been seated and was waiting for me at the table. As I approached, the first words out of my mouth were, "Wine. I need wine, now." (Was I drinking more wine lately?) She seemed almost as nervous as I was. "I was starting to worry about you," she said. 'With good reason,' I thought.

That evening I felt physically exhausted and the emotional stress of this next big step suddenly added to my anxiety and feelings of being over-whelmed. All those voices that talked to me in my head were speaking again. Some of the voices were screaming, 'You don't want to do this! What have you gotten yourself into?' Or whispering, 'This is harmless and perhaps it's time to meet a nice guy. You deserve a little happiness.'

I faced the fact that my wedding band had to be cut off when I walked into the jewelry store a few days later where both Dave and I had purchased jewelry and had rings resized. Six months ago this jeweler had made a diamond pendant for me from some of my mother's diamonds. That piece was gone now, too. The thieves had it.

I held my left hand out for the jeweler and, as he slipped a cutting wheel under my wide wedding band and started cutting, a sob caught in my throat. When he stopped, a fine, thin line had been cut through the band. *This band of gold that would last forever. This circle with no beginning and no end from then to now.* He used a plier-type instrument and spread the thin line until it was wide enough to allow me to slip my finger out. I was a little concerned that the cut had gone through the inscription Dave had engraved in it years ago. As it turned out, the jeweler's cut was exactly opposite the inscription and evenly spaced. How I held onto this little gesture of kindness from the universe!

The associate who was standing by watching this operation moved a magnifying glass in front of me and handed my ring to me. My spirit flew to that day when I sat on my front deck with friends and the coroner handed me Dave's wedding ring. I held the ring under the magnifying glass and read the inscription. It was still visible even after all the years of wear. *Sue Love Dave 9-2-1967*. I cried.

Once home, and as I settled in for the evening, thoughts of everything that had and was happening in my life filled my head. Having the ring cut off was not an abandonment of my love for Dave. The ring was too small and it had to come off so I could have it resized. I will still be able to wear it, and it will be a *circle of gold* once again.

In the meantime, I received a call from the dating service asking more questions about what kind of guy I'd like to meet. Now I was getting cold feet about going out on a date. Advice from friends: *just go and have a good time.* More advice: *don't think too much, just go.*

Two weeks passed before I heard back from the agency and they were now ready to arrange my first date with a gentleman who seemed to share many of the same interests I have. They gave me a quick overview of Mr. X and I said I'd meet with him. As the date approached, my apprehension grew and grew. It had been forty-five years since I had dated and the dating service told me it would take a miracle to find someone special in just four meetings. Right or wrong, crazy or not, I thought I just might be due for a miracle.

Monopoly

When did living in the present seem right?
like Monopoly I've passed 'GO'
moved on life's broad path
three steps forward
lose a turn
ride free on the B&O Railroad
bring me back to 'home.'

Go around that board enough
in my new-found image
(boot, battleship, pup, race car)
changing shapes to fit each day's mood
drawing on 'community chest'
(helping hands)
get out of jail free
(buying more time)
finding my pace.

Winning doesn't seem the only game in town,
buying houses and motels in the sky
creating a new life to stepping past my past
moving into a game of change and chance
there's a reason Monopoly is a winner.
life is ever changing
step up, step past, step again
or live in the then.

Chapter XV
Yes. Thank You. More Please.

Have I wasted time? When Dave passed I was fifty-eight years old. Not young, at least not in the sense that I was the epitome of the saying, 'young and carefree,' but not so old to be considered 'over the last hill.'

Now as I find myself able to go past the past, I'm sixty-five years of age and I've been on dates set up by a dating service. The morning after the first date, I took a hard look at myself in the mirror. Why is it I perceive myself as if I were twenty, or thirty but not the actual age I wear on my face or body? I think the simple answer is one feels as old as one's spirit. Thank goodness! I started to second-guess my reasons and the wisdom of setting up these blind dates.

While this first date was enjoyable, it was not with someone who I thought would be a match for me. We chatted over dinner for two-and-a-half hours and it was nice. I enjoyed, for the first time in years, having a one-on-one dinner with a gentleman.

Then came a second date set up by the dating agency. Again, I had an enjoyable evening with a different gentleman who was interesting and with whom I had many things in common. We chatted about travel, art, our social lives and families. It was fun.

Was it worth the time, effort and money I expended to go on only a few dates that did not culminate in lasting romance or partnership? For me, the answer is 'yes.' Until I had ventured out a few times, a question loomed overhead—how did I feel about dating at my age and at this time in my life, a life that had become very full again? What I discovered was that dating is not something I will pursue whole-heartedly. Life will carry me on its own wave and in its own time. Not having a significant other in my life is not paramount to my happiness.

Waste of time? No. Some newly-planted flowers and trees in my garden have taken a long time to take root over the years of Dave's absence, and some blossoms seem to have never bloomed at all, but it wasn't for lack of watering or tending. However my life grows, stretches and reaches for fulfillment, it has been on my terms and with the hard work of grappling with both the pain of loss and the joy of living.

A poignant line from a movie jumped from the screen and landed in my ears and in my heart. 'Yes. Thank you. More Please.' A young woman whose life seems to be splattered with illness, wrong decisions, and people who take advantage of her, as well as those who love her, delivers the line. She has a secret admirer. He loves her deeply but she just can't seem to see past his slightly nerdy ways. In a quietly unforgettable scene he asks her to close her eyes and just listen to his voice. After much balking, she relents, closes her eyes and listens to this man tell her what an awesome, beautiful and loveable person she is. His words become music to her ears and when he is done she slowly opens her eyes. And, for the first time she sees him for the loving person he has become in her world. Her only response is, "Yes. Thank you. More please."

She seems to believe the universe would continue to bless her if she was truly grateful and she would receive more if she said, 'please.'

In my world of thorns and roses, my spirit responds to what I'm thankful for and what I want to have more of in my life. I say "Yes" to trips to the ocean with crashing waves and orange sunsets, to mountains with waterfalls splashing, glinting, and tumbling down in carefree abandon. "Yes" to dreams of Dave with hugs and cheering. "Yes" to life. "Thank you" to friends who pad my life with understanding and patience. "Thank you" to my sons, daughter-in-law and grandson for their love. "More Please!"

I have figured out, or perhaps more accurately stated, learned, much along the way. One of these things is that 'alone' is not a four-letter word. Missing my loved ones will always cause pain, but its partner, 'being alone' is not a life sentence to misery. In a way, I have learned to grow within this space of solitude and that has been an eye-opening phenomenon. The knowledge that I have had worth as a daughter, partner and parent is humbling but also joyous. It is also with great anticipation that I move forward finding worth in whatever life brings my way. While I am technically not part of a couple, and the word 'alone' may seem appropriate, it is within this new space where I must find value in my life.

As I complete this writing, it has been seven years since my loss, and my forty-fifth wedding anniversary is coming up in a couple of weeks. It has taken me all these years to take the next step to move past the past, and its outcome is the beginning of my future.

I intend to live each day being present to what the world is holding up for me to witness and experience. I will still have moments of quiet pain from loss because life is like a seesaw with both ups and downs. There will be days when thoughts of Dave are painful, but I know I won't linger with those emotions or they will swallow me up. There will be days when I will have to push thoughts of Michele to the side because there is no managing the tender wound of losing my daughter. But I also understand I have to adjust to the daily seesaw and

I must have a plan to live life to the fullest. A life to fulfill Dave's wish for me—Be Happy.

Gentle Breeze

A soft gentle breeze
caressed my shoulders
like smooth silk.

An angel's breath
lightly touched my heart
into sweet life.

Be Happy

Acknowledgments

Loving thanks to my editor, Kari
Kynard Ridge, for your diligent work
and unwavering friendship, support
and encouragement to 'get it out there.'

To Karen Mireau, founder of Azalea
Art Press, my heart-felt thanks for your
expertise, guidance and friendship.

To Dr. Pamela Rudd, Ph.D., many
thanks for always saying, "Yes," to
reading each re-creation of my manuscript and for your steadfast encouragement over the last eight years—even in
the face of my derailment.

Without my cousin, Arlene Beaman,
and all our days and evenings writing
together, trips to the ocean and art
days—this book would only be a
dream. I send you *Butterflies* and love.

To my sons, Mike and Matt, my
daughter-in-law, Kristen, and my
grandson, Max—thank you for the gift
you are in my life. I love you.

About the Author

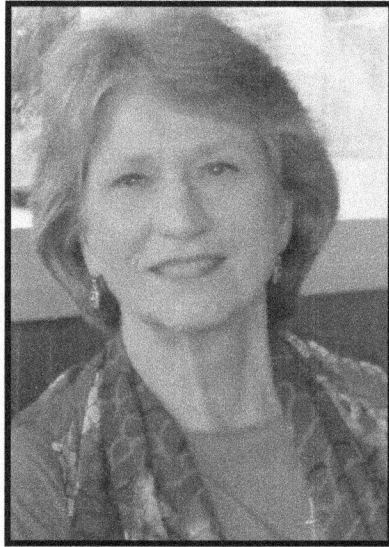

Susen I. Hickman was born in Oakland, California and has lived in the San Francisco Bay Area all of her life. She and her husband, David, raised three children—Michele, Mike and Matt—in Lafayette, California, where she still resides.

In addition to art, writing and music, Susen's interests include volunteer work with several organizations. She serves on the boards of directors of VoiceFlame, Inc., Soroptimist International of Diablo Vista, and East Bay Services to the Developmentally Disabled.

This memoir, seven years in the writing, is Susen's first book. She is currently working on a book of poetry.

www.ingramcontent.com/pod-product-compliance
Lightning Source LLC
La Vergne TN
LVHW011227080426
835509LV00005B/369